W9-CKQ-528

Euclid Public Library
631 East 222nd Street
Euclid, OH 44123
(216) 261-5300

Hitler's Alpine Retreat

Hitler's Alpine Retreat

James Wilson

CASEMATE

Philadelphia

Published in the United States of America
by
Casemate Publishers
2114 Darby Road
Havertown, PA 19083

Copyright © James Wilson, 2005

The right of James Wilson to be identified as Author of this Work
has been asserted by him in accordance with the
United Kingdom Copyright, Designs
and Patents Act 1988.

All rights reserved. No part of this publication
may be reproduced, stored in a retrieval system or transmitted,
in any form or by any means, electronic mechanical, photocopying,
recording or otherwise, without the prior permission of the publishers.
For additional information, contact Casemate Publishers,
2114 Darby Road, Havertown, PA 19083.

ISBN 1-932033-45-9

First edition, first printing

Cataloging in Publication Data is available
from the Library of Congress

Also published in Great Britain in 2005 by

Pen & Sword Books Limited
47 Church Street
Barnsley
South Yorkshire
S70 2AS

ISBN: 1-84415-263-4

Typeset in Optima by Pen & Sword Books Limited
Printed and bound in England by
CPI UK

Contents

𝕴𝖓𝖙𝖗𝖔𝖉𝖚𝖈𝖙𝖎𝖔𝖓

I n order to appreciate the importance of the Berghof (also called Haus Wachenfeld) and the role it played in the life of Adolf Hitler, we must go back to that point in time when Hitler first came to the area. On visiting Berchtesgaden and the Obersalzberg for the first time with his friend and mentor Dietrich Eckart, in mid 1923, he was 'completely captivated' by the region. Back in Munich and later that year, Hitler and the other Nazi leaders found themselves charged with high treason as a result of their unsuccessful attempt to seize power, (known as the Munich Beer-Hall 'Putsch') on 9 November, 1923. The authorities having suppressed the 'revolt' arrested Hitler two days later on 11 November. He was discovered while recovering from injuries received during the uprising at the family home of his friend, Ernst 'Putzi' Hanfstaengl in Uffing near the Staffelsee, some seventy kilometres (44 miles) south-east of the Bavarian capital.

Trials finally began in Munich on 26 February, 1924. Of the accused, the dominant figure would be Adolf Hitler. Thanks to powerful 'friends' in the Justice Ministry he was permitted to speak in his own defence and cross-examine various witnesses at length. Hitler seized upon the interest of the press who covered the event in depth not only in Germany, but around the world. Grasping the opportunity he displayed great oratorical prowess and political awareness in proclaiming the Party's ideas through his numerous 'speeches' during the trials. Furthermore, he highlighted the many 'injustices to' and 'sufferings of' the German people as a direct result of the unfair Versailles Treaty. Hitler emerged from the proceedings appearing victim, hero and patriot. He had turned defeat into victory by appearing on the front page of every newspaper in Germany and beyond. While reflecting upon the events of the trials Hitler later concluded that political success might be achieved without violent confrontation.

The sentence he received for his part in the Putsch was five years' imprisonment, that being the minimum penalty for a charge of high treason. However, once again due to lenient authorities and the intervention of 'friends in high places' the conditions he faced

OBERSALZBERG VOR DER ZERSTÖRUNG

in Landsberg prison were far from unpleasant. Hitler was now treated as something of a celebrity, to the extent that he was permitted to entertain friends in his own private room or wander around the prison gardens with his fellow inmates. Thus, with most of his time unoccupied he engaged himself in dictating the bulk of *Mein Kampf* (My Struggle) to his friend and fellow prisoner, Rudolf Hess. Having served only a small part of his five year sentence, Adolf Hitler was released on 20 December, 1924.

Following his release he returned to Berchtesgaden, spending time with friends and benefactors. Hitler's time was now occupied addressing small groups (although banned from such activity under the terms of his prison release) and dictating the second part of *Mein Kampf.* In 1927 destiny led Adolf Hitler to rent Haus Wachenfeld on the Obersalzberg. The house, typically Bavarian in style, offered fabulous views towards the Untersberg across the valley, and beyond into neighbouring Austria, the birthplace of the new tenant. The Obersalzberg is located a short distance from the town of Berchtesgaden. It is an area of outstanding natural beauty; here Hitler could relax, collect his thoughts and develop strategy for the continuing political struggle. Later, during the war, in reference to these early years on the Obersalzberg Hitler remarked; 'those were the best days of my life', praise indeed for someone whose domestic life prior to settling in the area had been somewhat turbulent.

Panorama of the Obersalzberg before the destruction.
This fabulous image shows the entire Nazi complex located on the Obersalzberg at the height of its development and following the completion of all building works. As the caption states, this is how the region appeared prior to the air raid on the morning of 25 April, 1945, which resulted in the destruction of many of the buildings seen here.

The identification of the buildings relates to the numbers as they appear on the original image; 1. Post Office in the prohibited area. 2. Nursery. 3. Chauffeur's living quarters. 4. Large garage. 5. Gatehouse to prohibited area. 6. Barracks/Economics building. 7. Barracks/Drill hall of bodyguard. 8. Parade ground/Underground shooting range. 9. Barracks/Living quarters. 10. Platterhof Hotel. 11. Platterhof Hotel staff living quarters. 12. Obersalzberg administration. 13. Model house for architectural planning. 14. Kindergarten. 15. Berghof. 16. Reich's security service and Gestapo.

Adolf Hitler was appointed German Chancellor on 30 January, 1933. The purchase of Haus Wachenfeld which had been agreed in September, 1932, was completed in late June, 1933. Using personal funds from the sales of *Mein Kampf,* Hitler had secured the property for a sum of around 40,000 gold marks. This single, unremarkable act, would ultimately lead to great changes in the area as the Berghof (mountain estate) was born. Hitler had become a wealthy man; *Mein Kampf* had been made compulsory purchase under new legislation. In addition and as head of state, he received royalty payments due to the fact that his face now appeared on postage stamps.

Haus Wachenfeld now underwent several stages of renovation and reconstruction, most of which were planned and paid for by Hitler himself. The Nazi Party then moved to persuade the Bavarian authorities to donate pieces of land in the immediate area towards the development of the newly planned complex. This, together with the compulsory purchase of farmland adjoining that of the Führer's property formed an enclosed area of some ten square kilometres at its conclusion. Initially, and on Hitler's instructions, these purchases were carried out correctly and generously. However, as time passed and with the involvement of Martin Bormann, reluctant landowners faced a stark choice; accept payment, or the concentration camp. The entire Obersalzberg now underwent dramatic change; the once peaceful farming area became a large, well ordered and well guarded estate. Of this area, Hitler personally owned only Haus Wachenfeld and the grounds in which it stood.

Throughout the early years during the many periods he spent on the Obersalzberg, Hitler enjoyed an almost carefree lifestyle. Here, in peace and comfort he could escape the daily grind of political administration and public duties, which he disliked. The Führer delighted in long walks in the region, with almost daily visits to his private tea house at Mooslahnerkopf in the valley below Haus Wachenfeld where he entertained selected guests. In these surroundings, Adolf Hitler projected an image of someone who loved nature and the great outdoors, a man of the people who enjoyed a simple and informal

Panorama of the Obersalzberg after the destruction.
In comparing this image with the previous postcard on pages 6 and 7, we can see the devastation inflicted upon the region in 1945 is almost limitless.

OBERSALZBERG NACH DER ZERSTÖRUNG

lifestyle. When in the company of ladies he was always extremely polite, the perfect host who amused everyone with his sharp sense of humour. Between 1923 and 1936, Hitler might spend as much as six months of the year on visits to his beloved mountain retreat.

The Obersalzberg had become a place of pilgrimage, literally thousands of people arrived on an almost daily basis. These adoring multitudes from every corner of the Reich wanted to see the place where their Führer lived, and perhaps, as was sometimes the case, be greeted by Hitler personally close to Haus Wachenfeld. After 1934, the masses were no longer permitted unrestricted access to the Obersalzberg, although the number of visitors to Berchtesgaden itself continued unabated. After that time the entire mountain became a more heavily restricted, high security area. In the end only those possessing special permits had access to the Obersalzberg, with no less than three checkpoints having to be passed before entering the central zone. Other members of the Nazi hierarchy, including Hermann Goering and Martin Bormann then set about acquiring their own property on the mountain close to the Führer.

From the day Hitler became Chancellor, the Obersalzberg and surrounding area assumed much higher status in the Nazi realm. The region was evolving to become Hitler's second seat of government; when not in Berlin it was on the Obersalzberg that the Führer made his decisions. It is therefore hardly surprising that major development followed. From 1936 and, under Martin Bormann's supervision many grand projects were undertaken, including a new road leading from the town of Berchtesgaden up to the estate. In addition many new buildings were constructed on the mountain to enhance the lifestyles of those who spent time in and around the Berghof, providing food, recreation and security, (including a huge SS barracks). Hitler's private residence also underwent major redevelopment during the period 1935/36. The new Berghof which was constructed around Haus Wachenfeld was indeed something worthy of the Führer, large and tastefully furnished, yet not ostentatious. It was here that Adolf Hitler entertained 'invited guests'; these included royalty, foreign heads of state and diplomatic envoys. On the other hand, if 'summoned', rather than 'invited' to the Berghof, an individual might be forgiven if harbouring any doubts as to the degree of hospitality they might expect upon arrival.

This period of massive construction on the Obersalzberg produced the large SS complex, kindergarten, chauffeur's quarters, garages, economics building, the huge Platterhof Hotel, administration buildings and much more. At the same time in the vicinity of Berchtesgaden itself more buildings were already appearing; these included a Reichs Chancellery, youth hostel, enormous army barracks and a new railway station. A small airport constructed at Ainring near Freilassing in 1933, served many who travelled to see the Führer on the Obersalzberg; upon arrival at the airport visitors were then chauffeur driven the remaining relatively short distance, about thirty-five kilometres (twenty-two miles) to Hitler's residence.

Throughout the war years Adolf Hitler made repeated visits to his mountain retreat, enjoying the peace and relaxation he had always found there. In 1943, with the increased fear of air-raids in the area it was decided to build a system of underground bunkers on the Obersalzberg. These vast excavations through solid rock, although never quite completed, were a remarkable undertaking. The bunkers themselves provided comfortable living quarters and ample store-rooms. They were supplied with water, electric power, communications and heating and ventilation systems, everything necessary to withstand a prolonged attack. An extensive network of tunnels, all with fortified entrances connected these bunkers, while externally anti-aircraft positions were improved and numbers increased.

On the morning of 25 April, 1945, with most of the Nazi leadership then in Berlin, some 318 Allied aircraft dropped approximately 1,230 tons of bombs on the Obersalzberg, causing extensive damage to the vast majority of buildings situated there. Just five days later, on 30 April, the Führer committed suicide in his Berlin bunker. Within a week of Hitler's demise the war in Europe ended, on 6 May, 1945. After the Second World War some of the less severely damaged buildings on the Obersalzberg were repaired, and taken over by the US military. In 1952 the bomb damaged remains of the Berghof were demolished. The Bavarian State only regained control of the mountain area following the departure of the Americans in 1995.

Today, a new documentation centre stands near the former site of the Platterhof Hotel; this provides an audio-visual history of the area during the Third Reich. Visitors to the centre also have an opportunity to enter part of the aforementioned tunnel/bunker system. Another section of this system can be entered through the delightful Hotel zum Türken, a traditional, family owned hotel established in the early 1900s. Due to its proximity to Hitler's residence, this property was confiscated by the Nazis in 1933 and used to accommodate the *Reichsicherheitsdienst* (Reich's Security Service), which was responsible for Hitler's personal security. Not until 1949 and under unique circumstances were the original owners permitted to reclaim the property; following repairs and refurbishment the hotel re-opened for business in late 1950.

When one considers that the Third Reich lasted little more than twelve years and, for the latter half of that period the regime was engaged in world conflict, the amount of construction carried out on the Obersalzberg and surrounding area alone between 1936 and 1942, almost defies belief. The execution of these large scale building programmes in themselves, clearly indicates the importance of the region to the Nazis, yet more so their Führer, Adolf Hitler, as his spiritual retreat and southern headquarters.

Despite the enormity of the projects undertaken in the area during the Third Reich and, the equally devastating efforts of the Allies to destroy those projects, the Obersalzberg and Berchtesgaden retain their almost magical charm; both remain as popular and beautiful today as they ever were.

Visitors to the Berghof

The following is a list of some of the visitors to Hitler's residence on the Obersalzberg. The fact that these individuals were received at the Berghof indicates the level of status the area had achieved under the Nazis.

1936   David Lloyd George, former British Prime Minister.
Count Galeazzo Ciano, Italian Foreign Minister, and Mussolini's son-in-law.

1937   Prince Aga Khan, leader of the Ismaili Muslims.
Duke (formerly King Edward VIII) and Duchess of Windsor.
Lord Halifax, British Foreign Minister.

1938   Kurt von Schuschnigg, Austrian Chancellor.
Neville Chamberlain, British Prime Minister.
André François-Poncet, French Ambassador.
Crown-Prince Umberto of Italy.
General Hiroshi Oshima, Japanese Ambassador.
Jacques Davignon, Belgian Ambassador.
Carol II, King of Romania.

1939   Colonel Józef Beck, Polish Foreign Minister.
Count Galeazzo Ciano, Italian Foreign Minister.
Sir Nevile Henderson, British Ambassador.

1940   Ion Gigurtu, Romanian Prime Minister.
Mihai Manoilescu, Romanian Foreign Minister.
Bogdan Filoff, Bulgarian Prime Minister.
Ivan Vladimir Popoff, Bulgarian Foreign Minister.
Monsignor Josef Tiso, President of Slovakia.
Bela Tuka, Slovakian Prime Minister.
Count Galeazzo Ciano, Italian Foreign Minister.
Maria José, wife of Crown-Prince Umberto of Italy.
Ramón Serrano Suñer, Spanish Foreign Minister.
Boris III, King of Bulgaria.
Alexander Cinkar-Marcovitch, Yugoslavian Foreign Minister.

1941   Bogdan Filoff, Bulgarian Prime Minister.
General Ion Antonescu, Romanian Prime Minister.
Benito Mussolini, Italian leader and Count Ciano, Italian Foreign Minister.
Dragisha Cvetkovic, Yugoslavian Prime Minister.
General Hiroshi Oshima, Japanese Ambassador.
Paul, Prince Regent of Yugoslavia.
Admiral Jean-François Darlan, Minister of Marine, Vichy France.
John Cudahy, US Ambassador to Belgium.
Ante Pavelic, Croatian Head of State.

Others include;
Count István Csáky, Hungarian Foreign Minister.
Nurenjev, Soviet Ambassador.
Cyrill, Prince of Belgium.
Pierre Laval, French Prime Minister (puppet government under Germany, 1942-44).

After 1941 the number of visits made to the Obersalzberg by those representing other countries became progressively less, as the need for diplomacy steadily diminished. Klessheim Castle near Salzburg then served as an alternative venue for diplomatic encounters until mid 1944.

Nonetheless, Hitler continued to receive his military commanders and other Party leaders at the Berghof during that time. In general terms from mid 1944 until the end of the Second World War, it was only those individuals from within Hitler's 'inner social circle' who spent much time on the estate, where daily life continued in an almost 'normal' fashion.

Propaganda Postcards

The use of postcards for patriotic and propaganda reasons, in so far as Germany is concerned, dates from the early 1900s. The introduction of faster photographic techniques and production methods at that time permitted the distribution of postcards on a scale as never before. During the First World War, many firms (including the famous W. Sanke of Berlin) produced large numbers of posed studio images in postcard form depicting many of Germany's better known, high ranking military figures.

The arrival of the latest technological advances in military hardware, such as aircraft, U-boats and airships into that conflict, contributed to the production of numerous postcards publicizing the new generation of young military hero. These were the men gaining fame and honour at what was then the 'cutting edge' of modern warfare. The availability of these postcards throughout Germany created an interest in collecting the sharp photographic images resulting from the latest processes.

Later, in 1933 when the Nazis came to power, the value of using postcards for

The Führer in front of his country house on the Obersalzberg.
Adolf Hitler, idolized Chancellor of Germany accompanied by his aides creates something approaching hysteria as he walks along the road near his beloved Haus Wachenfeld. Large crowds such as this were a common sight on the Obersalzberg in the early days; young and old with arms outstretched salute their Führer in an almost uncontrolled burst of enthusiasm.

propaganda purposes was fully realized and consequently used to maximum advantage and effect. The Propaganda Ministry of Dr Josef Goebbels was highly efficient; it had been determined that the postcard image could be personal, even intimate and strong in human interest. Here was a medium that could influence and inspire. With this in mind, the gargantuan machine that was the Propaganda Ministry went into overdrive, producing images of popular figures both political and military.

There followed a fantastic number of postcards showing the then rapidly expanding armed forces on manoeuvres with the latest equipment. So great was the interest that many military units were assigned their own photographer. These men were obliged to submit their work to the Propaganda Ministry where all images were selected and approved prior to production and release. If not selected for use as a postcard image the work of the unit photographer often found its way onto the pages of one or more of the many popular military magazines or newspapers of the day. Publications such as; *Der Adler* (the air force magazine), *Die Kriegsmarine* (the naval magazine),

Munich – The House of German Art.
Franz Triebsch, the Führer's painter.
This study of the Führer completed in 1941 depicts Hitler as the determined and charismatic military leader. The original painting was exhibited in the House of German Art in Munich; here it is yet another example of Hoffman's work to produce postcards from original works of art.

Die Wehrmacht (combined armed forces magazine), *Das Schwarze Korps* (the SS magazine) or *Signal* (the largest selling wartime picture magazine in Europe, also under the control of Dr Goebbels) featured much of the work of these men.

Military, patriotic and politically motivated postcards were widely available throughout the Third Reich with outlets on virtually every street corner. The Nazi Party had a ready source of revenue through this medium, in addition to the almost unimaginable propaganda value it provided. Many such postcards were distributed in other countries through the various German embassies before the Second World War, thus many examples turn up bearing foreign stamps and postmarks.

On the political side it has to be said production was almost limitless, particularly where Hitler himself was concerned. Of all political and military figures of the twentieth century, Adolf Hitler probably remains the single, most photographed and filmed personality of all. Many such images (some the work of Hoffmann, Hitler's personal photographer) then reproduced in postcard form depict Hitler in incalculable situations and locations, for example speaking at rallies, meeting the people, with other heads of state, in his Berlin Reichs Chancellery, or relaxing at the Berghof. The variety is staggering. As with the majority of German postcards of the period these are high quality photographic prints and not, as one might imagine, machine printed examples, (these do exist, but on a lesser scale).

The idea that Germany's infrastructure had been completely destroyed in 1945 through Allied 'saturation bombing' is open to challenge, in so much that all the materials and equipment necessary for the production of postcards were still in place, right up until the last days of the war. Unit photographers were still in a position to acquire film, to have that film processed, to obtain photographic paper for printing and return the work to Berlin for approval.

In retrospect this, combined with the fact that the government departments responsible for the design and production of new postage stamps were still operating, now seems inconceivable. This indicates that quantities of paper were available, electric power was in place and printing machinery functional. The idea that such things had been maintained at a time when priorities surely lay elsewhere, shows just how detached these bureaucrats were from the reality around them. That said, it also reveals how much emphasis had been placed on the postcard image, the believed effect it had in inspiring ordinary people and subsequently its contribution to maintaining a nation's morale.

The Nazis utilized this medium with great dexterity to promote strength, a political idea and a way of life, using intensive and invasive propaganda techniques that were very much ahead of their time. Many of their methods of political campaigning and use of the media for electioneering purposes have been adopted by numerous post war politicians around the world. No other nation had come to recognize the potential or appeal of the postcard image for purely propaganda purposes during that period.

Nevertheless, it must be said that other countries did produce patriotic postcards. However they had little impact and were never produced on such a scale as in Hitler's Germany. We must conclude therefore, on the evidence of the remaining postcards from the Nazi period, that the quantity and variety of these images together with the demand for them, even by today's standards, was almost inexhaustible.

Section One

Humble Beginnings

Postcard numbers 1 to 5 deal with the early life of Adolf Hitler, his family, where he was born and how these things were later used to deliver the idea of Hitler, the man of humble origin who knew hardship and pain, but who, having ultimately triumphed, remained a man of the people.

Klara Hitler

1. Mother of the Führer.

Klara Hitler, was probably the most important female figure in the life of Adolf Hitler. He was her favourite and she, the mother he adored. This postcard shows the distinct physical resemblance between mother and son; Hitler certainly inherited his mother's piercing gaze. Klara Pölzl was born in Spital, about seventeen kilometres (eleven miles) south of Gmünd, on 20 August, 1860. The families of both Hitler's parents had their origins in the Waldviertal region of Lower Austria; this rural wooded landscape inhabited mainly by peasant farmers at that time is located approximately 140 kilometres (88 miles) north-west of Vienna. The Führer's mother has been described as quiet, polite and hard working; when aged twenty she entered domestic service in Vienna.

On 7 January, 1885, she married Alois Hitler (1837-1903), her second cousin. This was not an uncommon occurrence in the area at that time; however, an Episcopal dispensation had to be obtained before the marriage could take place. Alois Hitler was a difficult man, and the marriage was not a particularly happy one, but Klara did all she could to make a home for herself and her husband who worked as a customs officer along the Austrian-German border. They had five children together, three of whom died in childhood; Gustav 1885-87, Ida 1886-88, Adolf 1889-1945, Edmund 1894-1900 and Paula 1896-1960. Adolf, however, was her favourite. While the boy feared his father, who often put young Adolf in his place via word or belt, or both, Klara indulged her son to an extent.

Alois retired from the customs service in 1895 after which time the family lived in the vicinity of Linz. Hitler's father, having suffered respiratory problems for some time, died as the result of a lung haemorrhage on 3 January, 1903, whereupon the family moved to Urfhar, a suburb of Linz. Klara, herself not a particularly strong or healthy person, had developed breast cancer. Hitler, who was in Vienna, on learning that his mother was now terminally ill immediately returned home to be by her side. Klara spent the last weeks of her life being lovingly nursed by her devoted son; she died on 21 December, 1907.

Hitler was absolutely devastated by the death of his mother; the bonds between them had always been very strong. Klara Hitler was laid to rest beside her husband in the small graveyard at Leonding. Hitler would spend the next five years wandering aimlessly around Vienna, until rescued from depression and obscurity by the outbreak of the First World War. Years later, following Nazi electoral success in 1933, further visits of the Führer to the graves of his parents in the quiet graveyard near Linz received the usual accompanying publicity, portraying the dutiful son paying his respects. Hitler's only surviving sibling, Paula, made her home in Berchtesgaden after the Second World War where she lived quietly until her death on 1 June, 1960. She is buried in Berchtesgaden's Bergfriedhof cemetery, where her final resting place remains carefully tended.

Alois Hitler

Alois Hitler, the father of the future German Chancellor was born in the village of Strones in Lower Austria, on 7 June, 1837, the result of a liaison between one Johann Georg Heidler, a miller, and Maria Anna Schicklgruber, a peasant girl. The names 'Heidler' and 'Hitler' (a later form of spelling the family name) actually sound very similar when spoken, which may account for early spelling variations and inaccuracies. The couple married five years later in May, 1842, at Döllersheim, but it was not until 1876, when he was almost forty years old, that the birth of Alois Schicklgruber would be legitimized; henceforth Alois would use the family name of Hitler.

Having served an apprenticeship as a cobbler, Alois then eighteen, left the area and joined the Imperial Customs Service near Salzburg. Thereafter he spent most of his working life serving as a customs officer in and around the area of Braunau am Inn, in Lower Austria. By 1875 Alois Schicklgruber had risen to the rank of Inspector of Customs, a supervisory position bringing responsibilities and, elevating the former peasant's son into the lower middle classes.

The Führer's father, while carrying out his duties both honestly and efficiently was popular with colleagues and superiors alike. It must be said that, given his background, Alois had actually done extremely well for himself in a world then dominated by a strict social class system.

2. Father of the Führer.

Alois Hitler would marry three times during his lifetime; in 1864 he married Anna Glasl-Hörer, the daughter of a fellow customs official. Anna was fourteen years older than Alois and the relationship was not a particularly happy one ending in legal separation in 1880. Following a long illness Anna died in 1883. A month later, Alois married again; Franziska Matzelsberger, a hotel cook, had already borne him a child Alois Jr., outside wedlock in 1882, then Angela in 1883 shortly after they were married. Sadly, within a year Franziska had succumbed to tuberculosis.

On 7 January, 1885, and, as previously discussed, having acquired the necessary Episcopal dispensation required for a marriage between second cousins, Alois married for the third and last time. Klara Pölzl and Alois Hitler were married in the Pommer Inn at Braunau am Inn, the very building in which Klara would give birth to her third child Adolf, on 20 April, 1889. Alois retired from the customs service in 1895 to receive a pension on which the family could live fairly comfortably. Unable to settle and, finding retirement difficult, Alois and family moved several times, finally settling in the village of Leonding just outside Linz.

The father of the future German Chancellor was an obstinate and unsympathetic man and his relationship with young Adolf was not a happy one, the latter often bearing the brunt of his father's displeasure by way of beatings. While perhaps sounding brutal, this was common practice at the time; the belief 'spare the rod and spoil the child' was one practiced by many. The fact that Alois could not settle, nor make a success of farming during his retirement may have added to an already strained relationship between the former customs official and his rebellious son; that, together with his occasional bouts of heavy drinking would have led to even more domestic disharmony. When young Adolf declared that he wished to pursue the life of an artist, his father, who was planning a life for his son as a civil servant, reacted in the usual way.

17

Klara, who had always cared for the two children from her husband's previous marriage as if they were her own, having already lost two children herself, Gustav 1885-87, and Ida 1886-88 before Adolf was born, may have overcompensated by lavishing too much attention of the young Adolf.

On 3 January, 1903, while taking his usual morning walk, Alois Hitler, having just entered his local tavern, Gasthaus Stiefler, complained of feeling unwell and died almost immediately of a pleural haemorrhage. He was buried in the quiet churchyard within sight of the family home two days later. Adolf Hitler, then almost fourteen, reportedly broke down and wept bitterly on seeing his father's body; the unrelenting struggle between domineering father and rebellious son was finally at an end.

3. The room of Adolf Hitler's birth in Braunau am Inn (Upper Austria).

It was in this room that Klara Hitler gave birth to her son Adolf, on 20 April, 1889.

While obviously celebrated by his immediate family, the event of Hitler's birth was otherwise without significance. It is therefore reasonable to assume, that this photograph if contemporary, would have been taken for other reasons, or at a later date; consequently we cannot be certain that the room appears exactly as it would have done in April, 1889.

4. Braunau am Inn, Salzburger Vorstadt.

Braunau am Inn, a small Austrian town close to the German border. The house on the right, Gasthof Josef Pommer, 15 Salzburger Vorstadt, is where Adolf Hitler was born at 6.30 on the evening of 20 April, 1889. Apart from the introduction of modern traffic etc., the scene remains virtually unchanged.

5. Braunau am Inn, Adolf Hitler's birthplace.
As Hitler achieved political success it was inevitable that the place where he was born would also acquire status. Here we see the building adorned with flags and Party symbols. To the left of the doorway stands an SS man, on the right a member of the SA.

Creating the Führer

Postcard numbers 6 to 10 reveal something of the transformation of Adolf Hitler from that rather awkward individual, obviously not at ease in front of the camera, to that point where his persona almost leaps from the image grasping the viewer's attention. Hitler had worked hard on these problems, these imperfections in the image he wished and needed to project together with his personal photographer, Heinrich Hoffmann. The results, over a relatively short period of time were staggering. Postcards such as these played no small part in creating the belief that in Hitler the German people had found a strong leader, one who would improve their lives in so many ways. These simple postcards projecting Hitler as the consummate political leader, gave little indication of the effort involved in their creation, or their true intention. A form of propaganda used so skilfully by the Nazis that its impact was neither apparent, nor accurately assessed during the period of the Third Reich; only when the regime had passed away would its influence be fully understood.

6. Reich Chancellor Adolf Hitler.

While lacking the impact of later examples, this rather gloomy study of Hitler was probably photographed soon after his having been elected Reich Chancellor. The Führer's unsurpassed popularity reached its zenith during the 1930s. Hitler's appeal transcended traditional class divisions still very much in existence at that time attracting support from a complete cross-section of society; workers, intellectuals and the upper classes, even to members of the German royal family offered their allegiance.

Crown Prince Wilhelm openly supported Hitler during the 1932 presidential elections and Prince Auguste Wilhelm, another of the Kaiser's sons, joined the Nazi Party in 1930, later serving as a *Gruppenführer* (Lieutenant-General) in the SS. Having witnessed Communism's rough attempts to establish itself in Germany, many of the nobility became alarmed at the prospect of such ideology winning popular approval. These genuine fears influenced the decision of many of the aristocracy, amongst them Prince Philip von Hessen, nephew to the Kaiser and grandson of Queen Victoria, to support Hitler.

On one hand, world economic depression and crippling reparations resulting from a particularly harsh Versailles Treaty coupled with inept German government; on the other, Hitler's personal magnetism, charisma and a gift of brilliant oratory combined with an ability to exploit and make political profit from the least opportunity. These explosive ingredients, together with a mastery of previously unseen and innovative electioneering tactics would see Adolf Hitler elected, and appointed German Chancellor on 30 January, 1933.

It is well known that Edward, Prince of Wales, later King Edward VIII harboured Nazi sympathies. Edward abdicated (in part forced upon him, in part self-inflicted) on 11 December, 1936, in favour of the woman he loved, Mrs Wallis Simpson. On 22 October, 1937, both visited Hitler at the Berghof then as Duke and Duchess of Windsor. At the same time, powerful elements certainly still existed in England who would have preferred to see Edward on the throne rather than his brother George, who was generally perceived as lacking in both character and personality when compared with Edward. The suggestion has been put forward that had England been defeated during the Second World War, Edward would almost certainly have regained his throne and remained a close friend of Nazi Germany.

7. Reich Chancellor Adolf Hitler.
While not a particularly natural pose and looking rather uncomfortable, the calculated semblance
of authority has been achieved by wearing full uniform, together with a stern expression deliberately
directed away from the camera.

8. Uncaptioned.
An altogether much more self-assured and confident look. This Hoffmann study of the Führer reveals something of Hitler's intense mesmerizing gaze, a characteristic remarked upon by many who met him.

9. Reich Chancellor Adolf Hitler.
A most compelling image projecting the man of destiny. Hitler's expression and bold posture challenges the camera to capture the moment.

10. Uncaptioned.
Hitler reads the *Völkischer Beobachter* (Racist Observer); this was the official Party newspaper which had been acquired in late 1920. The headline reads; '*Large remembrance meeting in Lipper country today*'.

Munich: City of Struggle & Triumph

Postcard numbers 11 to 26 relate to those places having the greatest significance in Hitler's early political life, with the exception of Landsberg Prison, all were located in the Bavarian capital, Munich. From the Sternecker Bräustübl, where Hitler first encountered the German Workers' Party in September, 1919, (by July, 1921, less than two years later, Hitler had won the internal battle for control of the Party, by then renamed the NSDAP and emerged as its undisputed leader) to the impressive buildings constructed around the Königsplatz, the centre of Nazi power when victory had been achieved.

11. Foundation corner of the NSDAP in the Sternecker Bräustübl Munich.

The notice on the table states: 'At this table the Reich's Chancellor Adolf Hitler founded the NSDAP'. The Sternecker Bräustübl located in Sterneckerstrasse im Tal, near the Isartor (Isar Gate, fourteenth century) was indeed the birthplace of the National Socialist German Workers Party; it was here that Adolf Hitler's political life began on 12 September, 1919. This postcard shows that part of the building where the Party held its first meetings. Here the area has been set aside as a shrine to the founder and other leading Nazis.

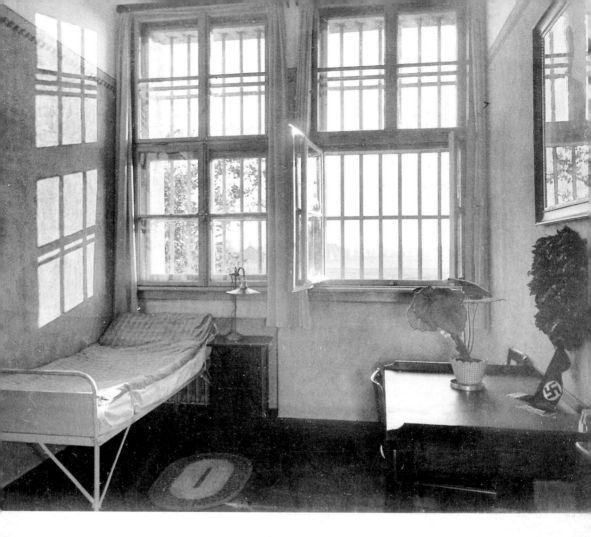

12. Adolf Hitler's cell in the prison fortress Landsberg am Lech.
Located on the first floor, room number seven is where Hitler served a small part of the five year
sentence he received for his role in the *Putsch* (revolt). His period of incarceration in Landsberg
prison began on 11 November, 1923, and ended on 20 December, 1924. During the time he spent
there Hitler was treated extremely well; he received visitors in his room and enjoyed unrestricted
access to the grounds. It was here, during the latter half of his sentence that he began to dictate
Mein Kampf, (My Struggle) to his fellow prisoners Rudolf Hess and Emil Maurice. On examining
this postcard a little more closely we can just make out a large picture of Hitler on the wall to the
right, below that a wreath with small Nazi drape attached.

13. Munich, Brown House.

Located at 45 Brienner Strasse and formerly known as the Barlow Palace, this building was acquired by the NSDAP in 1928 using Party funds and contributions from rich industrialists, particularly those of the Rhineland. Following internal alterations to Hitler's own ideas, the 'Brown House' opened as the new headquarters of the NSDAP at the beginning of 1931. The offices of Hitler, Hess, Goebbels and the SA were situated on the second floor; Hitler's office on the left side of the building overlooked the Königsplatz.

14. Munich, Brown House.

Another view of the Brown House, this time photographed from a point near the Königsplatz. On visiting the site today there is nothing to suggest that the building ever existed, no trace remains.

Münchén. Braunes Haus m. Führerhaus u. Ehre

15. Munich. Brown House with Führer House and Ehrentempel.

The Königsplatz; on the left stands the Führer House. To the right of the Führer House and on either side of Brienner Strasse (straight ahead) stand the Ehrentempeln, (temples of honour) these housed the remains of the sixteen comrades killed during the 1923 *Putsch*. The large building observed in the background between the Ehrentempeln is the Brown House. These imposing buildings around the Königsplatz were designed by Prof Paul Ludwig Troost (1878-1934). Troost was Hitler's favourite German architect, following the death of Troost in 1934, this honour passed to Albert Speer.

16. Munich, Ehrentempel for the fallen of 9 November, 1923.
Here we can see how the remains of those killed during the unsuccessful 1923 revolt were later housed within in the Ehrentempel. The words appearing on the top of each sarcophagus above the eagle and swastika read; '*Der Letzte Appell*' (The Last Parade), while the name of the individual appeared below the eagle in each case. The building standing on the right at the opposite end of the Königsplatz is the Propyläen, built in 1862; on the left stands the Antikensammlungen.

17. Munich. Brown House with Führer House and Ehrentempel.
A view across the Königsplatz and down Brienner Strasse towards the Obelisk in Karolinenplatz. It was along this stretch of the Breinner Strasse that many Nazi office buildings were located. By late 1939 the Party had over 6,000 people employed in this small area alone, the building on the right was the Verwaltungsbau der NSDAP (administration building of the Party). Beyond the Obelisk and at the other end of Brienner Strasse one finds the Feldherrnhalle. This particular image shows the buildings on either side of the street to be a perfect mirror image of each other, behind the Ehrentempel on the left stands the Brown House.

18. Munich. Führer House at Königsplatz.
Hitler's stylish Munich residence, the building remains unchanged and is located on Arcis Strasse near the junction with Brienner Strasse. Standing before the building today, now a school of music one can still make out where the fixing points that attached the large eagles to the façade above the doors were located. The structures observed on the right of the image with large columns are the Ehrentempeln.

19. The Führer House photographed in 2004 remains unchanged; today it is the *Staatliche Hochschule für Musik* (State High School for Music). The Ehrentempeln, (seen clearly in postcards numbers 15 and 17) constructed as a final resting place for the fallen comrades of 1923, these temples of solemn remembrance for the Nazis, have long since disappeared.

München, Mahnmal in der Feldherrnhalle

20. Munich, Monument of Remembrance in the Feldherrnhalle.

The Feldherrnhalle (Hall of Heroes) in the centre of Munich stands as a memorial to Germany's military heroes. It was here on 1 August, 1914, before the Feldherrnhalle that Adolf Hitler, amidst a large crowd, witnessed the German declaration of war.

Two days later, on 3 August, he joined the 1st Company, 16th Bavarian Reserve Infantry Regiment, (also known as the List Regiment). Hitler served with distinction during the First World War winning the Iron Cross, no mean feat for an ordinary soldier. This postcard shows the monument later erected by the Nazis at that side of the Feldherrnhalle overlooking Residenzstrasse. It was placed there in honour of the sixteen comrades killed in a skirmish with police during the *Putsch* of 9 November, 1923. Effectively was this encounter near the Feldherrnhalle that stopped the revolt in its tracks.

After the Nazis came to power in 1933, a commemorative march took place through Munich on 9 November each year to honour the memory and sacrifice of those sixteen fallen comrades. The names of those killed during the event are as follows: Felix Allfahrth, Andreas Bauriedl, Theodor Casella, Wilhelm Ehrlich, Martin Faust, Anton Hechenberger, Oskar Körner, Karl Kuhn, Karl Laforce, Kurt Neubauer, Klaus von Pape, Theodor von der Pfordten, Johann Rickmers, Dr M.E.V. Scheubner-Richter, Lorenz Ritter von Stransky, Wilhelm Wolf. Large wreaths hang on the side of the Feldherrnhalle below the Nazi monument; an SS guard of honour completes the scene.

21. Munich – Feldherrnhalle – pigeon feeding.
The front of the imposing Feldherrnhalle as viewed from Odeonsplatz. On the left of the structure, as we look into Residenzstrasse, we can just make out the dark shape of the monument to the Nazi dead situated on that side of the Feldherrnhalle.

22. The Feldherrnhalle as photographed in 2004; apart from the obvious removal of the symbols of the regime there appears little to distinguish between this image and postcard number 21.

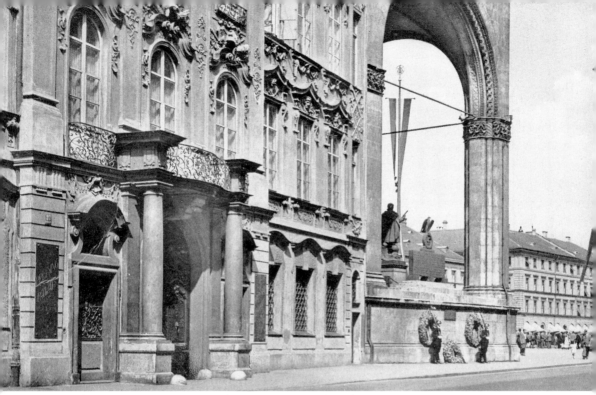

23. Munich. Preysing-Palace and Monument towards Odeonsplatz.
It was in this part of Residenzstrasse that the sixteen Nazis died in 1923, and here that the annual commemorative march including Hitler and other leading figures would come to a halt in solemn remembrance of those killed.

24. Munich. House of German Art.
Located on Prinzregentenstrasse near the junction with Königinstrasse, the House of German Art was designed by Hitler's favourite architect Albert Speer, together with considerable input from the Führer himself. It opened in mid 1937 with an exhibition of work by the best Nazi artists. The building remains unchanged and continues to perform the function for which it was originally constructed, a centre for the exhibition of art.

25. The historic meeting on 18 June, 1940 in Munich. Journey through the city.
A motorcade carrying Hitler and Mussolini having passed under the Karlstor makes its way through the city. Cheering crowds waving German and Italian flags line the route saluting the two leaders. France has been defeated; a matter of days later on 21 June, the Führer would deliver the terms of surrender to the French. On Hitler's instructions, the railway carriage in which the French had accepted the German surrender in 1918 was transported from its place in a Paris museum and, returned to the exact spot it had occupied twenty-two years earlier for that event in the Forest of Compiègne. The French were then forced to suffer a re-enactment of 1918; this time however, they were not the victors. In performing this action Hitler believed he had reversed the humiliation inflicted on the German nation at the end of the First World War, the much hated Versailles Treaty was finally laid to rest. Three days later, by order of the Führer the railway carriage was blown up.

26. The Karlstor today, compared with postcard number 25 it is obvious that many of the surrounding buildings have been renovated or replaced over the years, partly the result of wartime damage and simply the need to modernize. Munich, in keeping with other major cities in today's world moves continually forward.

Berchtesgaden: Fount of Inspiration

Postcard numbers 27 to 34 deal with the town of Berchtesgaden, a priceless jewel set in an emerald sea. On observing these images one can appreciate and fully understand why Adolf Hitler would choose this region to establish his country retreat. The indescribable rejuvenating essence of the area soothes and claims one's very soul on first contact; then, like some unseen irresistible force it continually draws the helplessly spellbound individual back unto itself, time and time again. Such may have been the effect of this region upon Hitler that, together with it being reminiscent of his native Austria lying across the nearby border, would have proved a combination too strong to resist.

27. Berchtesgaden.
The charming market town of Berchtesgaden. This early postcard probably dates from the 1920s and shows the town from an angle popular with photographers, in this instance the magnificent Watzmann dominates the background.

28. Berchtesgaden today, obviously there has been a degree of development in the area since postcard number 27 was produced, however, both images are comparatively similar in most respects and many features remain unchanged.

29. Uncaptioned.
Berchtesgaden in the full grip of winter, this card bears a postmark of 23.1.23; Hitler's first visit to the area in May later that year would leave a lasting impression on the future Chancellor. On his return to the region as Führer in the 1930s, it was Hitler who would leave a lasting impression on Berchtesgaden and the surrounding area.

30. Berchtesgaden Market Square with Watzmann.

Berchtesgaden's quaint market square, quiet and peaceful. In the background above the rooftops stands the mighty Watzmann. Bearing a postmark dated 12.9.42, the sender tells of their journey from Freilassing to Berchtesgaden by train, how warm the weather is and the wonderfully clear view of the mountains. Freilassing is close to the Austrian border and Salzburg; when travelling to Berchtesgaden by rail one changes trains at Freilassing.

31. The market square in 2004. The fact that this photograph was taken early on an October morning may account for the lack of tourists in this particular instance. Nonetheless, the two images are unmistakably the same market square. Given that over sixty years have elapsed since postcard number 30 was produced the differences between the two scenes remain minimal.

32. Market Square in Berchtesgaden.

Here we view the market square from the opposite side to that seen in postcard number 30. In this instance buildings stand adorned with flags and swastikas that appear to have been fashioned from the soft ends of pine branches. This image for whatever reason certainly dispels the idea of a town overflowing with Party faithful visiting the area so loved by their Führer. (One must accept that a period of several years may exist between the time of origination of an image and the date of the postmark; therefore any image may represent a different timeframe.)

37

33. Berchtesgaden with Watzmann.

A peaceful scene showing Berchtesgaden in autumn, chimney smoke drifts skywards and all trees stand bare save the evergreens. With a postmark of 16.9.41, the message on the reverse makes no reference to a war already entering its third year.

34. Berchtesgaden with Hochkalter.

The town as viewed from across the valley with the Hochkalter in the background. Posted on 14.8.41, the sender greets her friends referring to everyday things, the length of her journey, the weather and the stunning view of the Watzmann from her hotel.

Obersalzberg: Spiritual Retreat

Postcard numbers 35 to 40 show the Obersalzberg and surrounding countryside in the early years before the Nazi regime had completely taken over the area. At the time these images were recorded on film, neither the photographers, nor the residents of the homes depicted here, could have possibly imagined the scale of change soon to engulf this peaceful region; change so great it would alter both the landscape and their lives, totally, and forever.

35. Berchtesgaden, Obersalzberg towards the south.
The lower slopes of the Obersalzberg, a patchwork of small farms and rolling pastures, typical of the area prior to the mid 1930s. The town itself can just be seen on the extreme right of the image.

36. Obersalzberg near Berchtesgaden.
Another early scene, the house on the extreme right is Villa Bechstein which was situated a short distance down the valley from Haus Wachenfeld. The property was later acquired by the Nazis and following renovation used to accommodate visiting VIPs, including Goebbels and Mussolini.

37. Café Restaurant Steiner on the Obersalzberg.

This stylish restaurant was situated by the roadside a short distance below Haus Wachenfeld. Flying the flag did not prevent the owners losing this fine property; like so many located in the vicinity of Hitler's residence, it was demolished following the takeover of the mountain.

38. Hindenburg Hill. Obersalzberg with view towards Salzburg.

The central area of this image would later form the heart of Hitler's mountain estate. The building seen highlighted on the right was the home of Dr Richard Seitz. Purchased by Martin Bormann in 1936 and following extensive renovation, this property became the Bormann family home.

Izberg bei Berchtesgaden mit Landhaus Göring. Bayr. Hochland   9747 Mono

39. Obersalzberg near Berchtesgaden with Landhaus Goering. Bavarian Highlands.

This postcard clearly reveals the elevated position enjoyed by the Goering family home on the Obersalzberg in relation to other buildings in the immediate area. Landhaus (country house) Goering, seen standing in open ground on the right, offered commanding views over the entire region together with a level of privacy beyond that of other residents. The card bears a postmark dated 22.8.35. It was around this time that Haus Wachenfeld underwent its greatest transformation, a metamorphosis from which the Berghof would emerge. It was also around this time that Bormann began to express an interest in the home of Dr Richard Seitz.

40. Obersalzberg near Berchtesgaden, Bavarian Highlands.

The existence of the flag on the hilltop to the right indicates that Hitler was already Chancellor at the time this postcard was produced. This peaceful landscape, unchanged for generations, would soon undergo dramatic change as the Nazis introduced their ambitious plans for the area.

Haus Wachenfeld: A Country Home

The following photographs (numbers 41 to 49) have been selected from a series of half sized postcard images by Hoffmann; each series came in a small card packet containing twenty photographs. Hitler's immense popularity at this time dictated the production of these small, more personal images. It is reasonable to assume that such photographs depicting Hitler and other Nazi related subject matter were not only collected by individuals, but were given and received as gifts. Many of these same images are encountered in the usual postcard sizes.

41. View of the Untersberg from Haus Wachenfeld.
While framed in the doorway leading to the balcony on the first floor, Hitler looks out across the valley towards Austria. In the background stands the Untersberg.

42. Our Führer, the great friend of animals.

In feeding these small deer Hitler portrays the gentle image of a man in tune with nature. On Hitler's instructions, the landscape and all wildlife contained within the area of the Obersalzberg were to be preserved. Furthermore, he stated that all construction on the mountain should be unobtrusive in an attempt to maintain a degree of harmony with the natural surroundings.

43. Sun terrace at Haus Wachenfeld.

While bathed in sunshine Haus Wachenfeld's main terrace offered truly spectacular views towards the town of Berchtesgaden, the legendary Untersberg across the valley and, weather permitting, the city of Salzburg in neighbouring Austria.

44. View from the terrace of Haus Wachenfeld toward Berchtesgaden.
Hitler looks down o the Party faithful. Adoring crowds make their way alon the road below Hau Wachenfeld, their devotion rewarded the Führer appears on the terrace.

45. A little one's visit on Obersalzberg.
By engaging this endearing child in this attentive way, Hitler projects the image of a caring and approachable leader; a man truly in touch with his people. Nazi innovation involving the production of these seductive vote winning images has not been wasted on today's politicians; similarly, they too fully appreciate the appeal and importance of being seen and photographed in the company such delightful subjects.

46. View from Haus Wachenfeld towards the Untersberg.
Hitler, posing near the house, gazes thoughtfully across the valley in the direction of his birthplace, Austria.

47. 'Adolf Hitler Hill' on the Obersalzberg, (1000m above sea level).
Two young women give the unmistakable Nazi salute. They have reached a high point in the area
then known as 'Adolf Hitler Hill'. The strategically placed flag acts like a magnet attracting people
to the spot.

48. The Führer on Obersalzberg.
Hitler, in sitting alone on the perimeter wall of the terrace in this way, succeeds in communicating the idea of the somewhat solitary, pensive figure; it is he, and he alone, who must bear the weight of leadership.

49. The resting Führer with his faithful guard.
Hitler, the ordinary man enjoying life's simple pleasures, rests with his faithful companion. While this image might conjure such interpretation, the fact remains that Hitler had great affection for his dogs and always enjoyed walking on the Obersalzberg.

Postcard numbers 50 to 100 deal with Haus Wachenfeld, the unpretentious and traditional alpine cottage located on the Obersalzberg as purchased by Adolf Hitler on 26 June, 1933.

In covering various stages of renovation they reveal the improvements Hitler had carried out to the property prior to the almost complete remodelling programme of 1935/36. Thereafter the Führer's country residence would generally be referred to as, the 'Berghof'.

50. Obersalzberg (1,000m) towards Berchtesgaden and Adolf Hitler's country house Wachenfeld.
The Obersalzberg as viewed from a point close to the home of Dr Seitz, (later Bormann's house). In the foreground stands Hotel zum Türken, beyond that Haus Wachenfeld, while Berchtesgaden itself sits peacefully in the valley below. In the foreground on the extreme left is Marienhäusl, demolished after 1933 to provide part of the site for the kindergarten; above that again on the left is the Bodner farm, also later demolished.

Hoher Göll 2519

51. Obersalzberg – original aerial photo.
This unusual aerial view shows Haus Wachenfeld and that part of the Obersalzberg which later formed the heart of the restricted central area. The house has already undergone considerable redevelopment and would remain as seen here until the grand remodelling programme of 1935/36 produced the new Berghof. There are people visible on the road and by the gate, but strangely in this instance, the vast crowds are conspicuous by their absence. With the exception of Hotel zum Türken, observed just above and to the left of Haus Wachenfeld, all other buildings in this photograph would be demolished as the Nazis tightened their grip on the region.

52. Haus Wachenfeld on the Obersalzberg.
Another aerial view of Haus Wachenfeld and the Obersalzberg region, in this instance appearing somewhat insignificant against the backdrop of the magnificent Hoher Göll. The sprawl of buildings high on the left in open pasture is Pension Moritz, also called the Platterhof. On studying this image together with postcard number 51, it is evident that the area which later formed the Nazi central zone on the Obersalzberg and accommodated most of the buildings they erected following the takeover, was in fact, quite a small area.

49

53. Haus Wachenfeld Berchtesgaden – Obersalzberg.
This postcard dating from the early 1930s presents the house as it would have appeared to Hitler at the time he purchased the property in 1933. As yet there is no evidence of any renovation work having taken place; the area to the left of the house remains untouched while trees still grow close around the building.

54. Hitler's favourite place to stay in Berchtesgaden.
It is quite unusual to see Haus Wachenfeld presented from this particular angle. Photographed in the early 1930s it shows some of the farm buildings belonging to other inhabitants located close to, and just below, Hitler's residence; these along with many others in close proximity were later demolished. It was the view across the valley towards Austria that never failed to inspire Hitler, continually drawing him back to this magical landscape; this region, having once cast its spell, will not let you go.

55. Uncaptioned.
This early image sees a rather uncomfortable looking Hitler attempting to relax while on the Obersalzberg. Capable however of making any unwanted visitors feel even more uncomfortable, is his unnerving, ever-watchful companion.

56. The Hitler House, Obersalzberg near Berchtesgaden.
Haus Wachenfeld photographed in its original state, peaceful, traditional and possessing great rustic charm; as yet no work has begun.
The building glimpsed in the background, upper right, is almost certainly the home of Dr Richard Seitz. This property, occupying an elevated position that overlooked Haus Wachenfeld was bought by Martin Bormann in 1936 and rebuilt as 'Landhaus Bormann' to accommodate his own large family.

57. Chancellor Adolf Hitler in Berchtesgaden.
This early image with a postmark of 29.12.33 sees Hitler in the company of a small group standing before Haus Wachenfeld. The scene appears non-contrived, informal and relaxed; apparently surprised, the man on the right draws the group's attention to the presence of the photographer. In reality all photographs had to be submitted to the relevant department for inspection and approval prior to publication. Nonetheless, an unusual image for all that.

58. Residence of Adolf Hitler on the Obersalzberg near Berchtesgaden.
Haus Wachenfeld photographed from a point just below Hotel zum Türken looking towards the Reiteralpe. The modest pathway leading from the road to the house passes a small enclosed vegetable garden seen in the foreground on the right.

Führer mit R. Hess auf Haus Wachenfeld

59. The Führer with R. Hess at Haus Wachenfeld.
This interesting early postcard shows Hitler and his deputy Hess admiring the view from Haus Wachenfeld towards Berchtesgaden. Both men wear traditional Bavarian dress in what appears to be an informal get together. Rudolf Hess as a subject does not appear frequently in postcards; consequently an image such as this commands a high price.

60. The house of the Führer.
The renovation of Haus Wachenfeld gets underway. What would become the conservatory (also called the winter garden) is visible at an early stage of construction on the left at the front of the house. The whole scene resembles that of a building site; as such it is surprising this image was ever released, presenting the Führer's residence in a state of disorder.

61. Hitler Youth in front of the Führer's house on the Obersalzberg.
Flag-bearing Hitler Youth congregate on the road near Haus Wachenfeld while an SS man makes his way through the group in the direction of the photographer. Looking at the house itself it is obvious that further alterations are underway; the grassed slope below the conservatory has been removed to accommodate the newly constructed garage, while a temporary workmen's hut on the right has building materials stacked behind it.

62. View from Alpine Hotel zum Türken to Adolf Hitler's country house Wachenfeld and Reiteralpe Mountains (Obersalzberg 1,000m).
This pleasant and relaxed scene shows guests enjoying the view from the hotel terrace towards Haus Wachenfeld. This image gives a good indication of how near Hotel zum Türken actually was to the Führer's residence. The terrace provided an excellent viewing platform constantly used by those hoping to catch a glimpse of Hitler when he was on the Obersalzberg.

63. Photographed in 2004 and from a similar position to that of the previous postcard number 62, the former site of Haus Wachenfeld appears very overgrown and virtually unrecognizable. Part of the service road which led to the rear of the later constructed Berghof remains visible on the hillside in the lower foreground.

64. A little one's visit on Obersalzberg.
Possessing all the elements of an unexpected photo opportunity, the little girl chosen to be photographed with the Führer appears somewhat bewildered; Hitler on the other hand fully realized the appeal of such images. Do politicians ever change.

65. Reich Chancellor Adolf Hitler (standing right) on the terrace of his country house Wachenfeld entertaining a little girl from Berchtesgaden (Obersalzberg 1,000m).
Here the conservatory and garage mentioned in caption 61 are observed at close quarters. Tradesmen are working on the property and building materials lie scattered all around. Hitler, in the company of an unidentified man in uniform and a local child, surveys the scene from the terrace above; to the left of this group yet another man captures the moment on film.

66. Reich Chancellor Adolf Hitler in Berchtesgaden.
Hitler, Goebbels and Ernst 'Putzi' Hanfstaengl stand by the drive leading to Haus Wachenfeld. The open gates observed behind Goebbels were a temporary feature at the property and appear in very few images. Hanfstaengl met Hitler in late 1922 in Munich and, almost immediately became one of the Führer's 'inner circle' of friends. Hitler delighted in having Hanfstaengl play the piano for him, particularly pieces by Wagner. Hanfstaengl went to become the Führer's 'front man' in matters involving the foreign press.

67. Adolf Hitler's country house Wachenfeld seen from Alpine Hotel Türken.
Here we view Haus Wachenfeld and the outstretched valley below from the now extended terrace at Hotel zum Türken; again this image clearly demonstrates the close proximity of the two properties. In the end Hitler became irritated by the constant public attention he received from the hotel terrace due to its position. This led to ill feeling between the Führer and the Schuster family who owned the hotel, culminating in the property being confiscated in 1933.

68. We all want to give the Führer our hand.
While accompanied by members of the SS, a fatherly Hitler greets some children selected from the daily gathering on the road near Haus Wachenfeld. The taller girl on the left patiently awaits an opportunity to request the Führer's autograph on the postcard that she carries; quite customary on such occasions. In the background stands Hotel zum Türken.

69. Heartfelt Best Wishes for the New Year.

A scene of complete tranquillity, Haus Wachenfeld and the surrounding area rests beneath a blanket of deep snow. The photographer has skilfully used the natural light to produce a particularly enchanting image. Posted in Berchtesgaden in 1934, part of the message on the reverse reads; 'This is the home of our dear Führer Adolf Hitler'.

70. Our Führer's and Chancellor's home on the Obersalzberg.

A figure raises the flag in front of the house. Hundreds of people line the road leading to the property all hoping to see their Führer. Haus Wachenfeld has been renovated and extended; again it would remain as seen here until greatly enlarged in 1935/36 to become the new Berghof. Some of the original farm buildings in the area can be glimpsed through the trees, while on the extreme left is Hotel zum Türken.

71. A little visitor on Obersalzberg.

All lined up and smiling for the Führer, the young lady who has caught Hitler's attention was a regular visitor at Haus Wachenfeld and appears in a number of postcards with Hitler. The older girls in uniform are members of the *Bund Deutscher Mädel-BdM* (League of German Girls), an organization for German girls aged ten to twenty-one and organized similarly to the Hitler Youth. The BdM also came under the control of *Reichsjugendführer* (Reich Youth Leader) Baldur von Schirach. Behind Hitler stands his adjutant, Lieutenant Wilhelm Brückner of the SA.

72. Haus Wachenfeld, Obersalzberg.

Haus Wachenfeld photographed looking back towards the mountain road. A small group stand talking in front of the garage. Note the assertive posture of the man second from the left wearing a light coloured jacket and dark trousers; characteristically Hitler. If we compare this image (post-construction) with postcard number 60 showing the conservatory during initial construction, we can appreciate the scale of development to have taken place in this particular area.

Haus Wachenfeld, Obersalzberg.

och über den Wolken!
ichskanzler Adolf Hitlers Landhaus „Wachenfeld" a. Obersalzberg (1000 m)
gegen die Reiteralpe
1028

73. High above the clouds! Reich Chancellor Adolf Hitler's country house Wachenfeld on Obersalzberg (1,000m) towards the Reiteralpe.

Spot the difference; this image and postcard number 74 have been photographed from almost the exact same point. However, apart from the fact that low cloud completely obscures the valley in this particular instance, there are a number of differences between the two.

74. Haus Wachenfeld, the Führer's home on the Obersalzberg.

The cloud which cloaked the valley has dispersed and Haus Wachenfeld emerges from yet another series of minor alterations. When compared with postcard number 73 and, moving left to right, we see that the small additional room in the foreground has been completed, the chimney on the main roof has been built up, a screen has been added to the wall around the terrace, work has been done immediately left of the garage doors and a parking area has been created complete with flagpole. It is fair to say that from the time Hitler purchased the property until the 1935/36 redevelopment which produced the new Berghof, Haus Wachenfeld was subject to alterations of varying magnitude on an almost continual basis.

75. Haus Wachenfeld.

This photograph was taken from a point on the road where it joined the drive to Haus Wachenfeld. The gates were situated just a few metres from the roadside. This allowed vehicles to stop before the gates but safely off the road itself. The small sign by the fence reads; Haus Wachenfeld, entry forbidden, beware dogs!

76. The Führer's faithful guard Sirus at Haus Wachenfeld on Obersalzberg.

Hitler's dog, Sirus photographed close to Haus Wachenfeld. Sirus preceded Blondi, the German shepherd later presented to the Führer by Bormann. Hitler was undoubtedly a dog-lover. During the First World War he had adopted a small terrier, Fuchsl, and kept it in the trenches with him. Close examination of this photograph leads one to the conclusion that the image of the dog has been cleverly added to the original photograph at a later stage. German photographers were quite skilled in such techniques.

5228

77. The Führer at Obersalzberg.

Members of the Hitler Youth gather before the gates to Haus Wachenfeld. Each boy eagerly awaits his turn as the Führer autographs the postcards they have brought along. Meanwhile the lad on the right uses his camera to capture their special moment forever.

78. Reich Chancellor Adolf Hitler's Haus Wachenfeld - Obersalzberg.

An image of superb quality reflecting the simple charm of the Führer's mountain home, the one place he continually found peace and refuge from all the complications and pressures associated with statesmanship. Here he could relax and lead the simple life he often yearned for.

Der Führer und sein Stellvertreter Hess.

79. The Führer and his deputy Hess.
Hitler and Hess photographed on the drive near Haus Wachenfeld. While Hitler wears standard uniform his deputy is observed in traditional Bavarian attire. Following the flight of Hess to England in May, 1941, his successor Martin Bormann, 'the intriguer' attempted to remove any reminders and all traces of Hess; this extended to anything bearing the image of the former Deputy Führer. Consequently postcards such as this are to be considered quite rare.

80. Out of the visiting crowd at Obersalzberg.
Hitler chooses a little girl from the daily throng at the gates to Haus Wachenfeld. The child beams as she walks hand in hand with the Führer towards the house. Her family will be so proud and her friends so jealous of her great adventure.

81. Thank you for the birthday invitation.
The little girl seen in postcard number 80 appears again. The caption would suggest that the child has been invited to spend a short time with the Führer due to the fact that it's her birthday. The result is a touching image revealing Hitler's close relationship with children; this man of the people. Yet this photograph shows an intimacy rarely seen in many others. Unusually, the child is permitted to hug Hitler, whilst kissing him on the cheek. He clearly returns the embrace in response to her innocent affection.

Landhaus „Wachenfeld" im Berchtesgadener Land (Obersalzberg 1000 m)

Nr. 1025 Phot. H.

82. Hitler's country house Wachenfeld in Berchtesgadener Land (Obersalzberg 1,000m).

The almost daily procession past the Führer's residence was an act of faith for many of the participants; this truly awesome spectacle began in the late 1920s prior to Hitler being elected Chancellor and continued unabated throughout the early years. The frequency of these visits and the numbers involved were subject to strict control following restrictions introduced after 1934 denying the general public access to the area en masse.

83. The Führer in Berchtesgaden.

While accompanied by Hitler Youth Leader, Baldur von Schirach (standing behind Hitler) and Hermann Goering, head of the Luftwaffe (extreme right), the Führer engages his adoring public on the road close to Haus Wachenfeld. In the background we glimpse part of Hotel zum Türken.

84. Adolf Hitler's dwelling house on Obersalzberg near Berchtesgaden.
Reverse reads: The high Berchtesgaden health resort Obersalzberg.
Peaceful and picturesqu Haus Wachenfeld as viewed from the main terrace of Hotel zum Türken.
The Obersalzberg and surrounding area had long been considered a health resort due to the purity of the mountain air, particularly for thos with breathing ailments or in need of recuperation.

85. Haus Wachenfeld, country home of the Reich Chancellor in Berchtesgaden.
Looking up towards the Führer's residence from the lower slopes of the Obersalzberg. Although obviously extended, the building adheres to typical alpine styling thus allowing a high degree of harmony between structure and landscape.

86. Hitler's country house Wachenfeld towards Reiteralpe.
Another charming 'chocolate box cover' type study of the residence.
A number of vehicles stand on the parking area by the flagpole, including what appears to be a military staff car.

87. Moonlight at Hitler's country house Wachenfeld and Obersalzberg (1,000m).
A beautifully clear night on the Obersalzberg, the full moon casts its magic spell illuminating the entire area to conjure up this fabulous 'fairytale' type scene.
This particular postcard is a personal favourite; the photographer's patience has been rewarded and his professionalism has produced an image where the viewer can almost feel the seclusion and the stillness of the night.

88. Haus Wachenfel[d] country house of th[e] Reich Chancellor in[ ] Berchtesgaden.
Looking across the garden area towards the original main pa[rt] of the house, this postcard allows us t[o] appreciate just how much work has bee[n] carried out on the property when compared with earl[y] images showing this side of the residenc[e] for example postcar[d] numbers 53 and 56.

89. A little one's visit on Obersalzberg.
Hitler presents a gift to his little visitor on the terrace at Haus Wachenfeld. This same child appears with the Führer in postcards numbers 45, 71 and the next image number 90 perhaps she is the daughter of a local Party member. In any event she was a regular visitor who featured in a number of well planned photographic sessions.

[e]iner Besuch auf Obersalzberg

Besuch auf Obersalzberg

90. A little one's visit on Obersalzberg.
Again the Führer entertains the same young lady at his country residence. The reverse of this postcard bears a number of special postmarks celebrating the 1938 Reichs Party Day in Nuremberg. These huge rallies attended by Hitler and other members of the Party hierarchy consisted of endless marching columns of SA and SS and concluded with the usual speech making.

91. Haus Wachenfeld, country house of the Reich Chancellor in Berchtesgaden.
Photographed from a point uphill and almost behind the property, this image gives an indication of the distance to the mountains opposite and the spectacular views afforded on a clear day.

Saarkinder als Sommergäste
bei der Schwester des Führers auf Obersalzberg

Sie hat dem FÜHRER die Hand geben dürfen

92. Saar children as summer guests of the Führer's sister on Obersalzberg.

The Führer enjoys the company of two little girls from the Saar region who are spending time at Haus Wachenfeld as the guests of his half-sister Angela, his housekeeper from 1928 to 1936.

Contemporary accounts indicate that Hitler was genuinely fond of children; nonetheless, what respectable politician would turn down the opportunity to be photographed with these endearing subjects.

93. She has been allowed to give the Führer a hand.

These two little girls are so engrossed in their own activity that they seem oblivious to the Führer's presence. Having paused, Hitler observes his little guests as would some proud father during their walk near Haus Wachenfeld.

94. Haus Wachenfeld, country house of the Reich Chancellor in Berchtesgaden.

To say that Hitler's 'little place in the country' offered adequate views of the surrounding area would be something of an understatement; whether as Haus Wachenfeld, or the Berghof this was the magnificent uninterrupted view of the Untersberg opposite the Führer's residence on the Obersalzberg. The Untersberg is steeped in legend. It is said that the Emperor Charlemagne sleeps deep beneath the mountain and will return to save Germany in time of need. To have his country home situated overlooking the Untersberg which is part German, part Austrian, must have been a source of deep personal satisfaction for Hitler; from here he could see his native Austria and weather permitting, observe Salzburg and its castle.

95. Interior of Haus Wachenfeld, country house of the Reich Chancellor.

This interior view of Haus Wachenfeld was photographed in the early days when it was simply the Führer's country home. Unlike the later Berghof this was not a place to entertain and impress foreign dignitaries. Worth noting yet easily missed, is the small figure of a saluting Brownshirt above the lampshade.

96. Interior of Haus Wachenfeld, country house of the Reich Chancellor.

Here we view what is described as the living room. Cosy and unpretentious, this room was located to the right hand side of the main door to the house; it lay behind the bay window clearly observed in postcard number 78.

97. The Führer takes the favourable voting results on Obersalzberg.

Hitler takes a telephone call informing him of the outcome of the plebiscite on the disputed Saar region held on 13 January, 1935 (the area had been ceded to France in 1919 under the Versailles Treaty). With over 90 per cent of the electorate having voted for a return to Germany and the Reich it is small wonder that the Führer appears extremely pleased.

98. Haus Wachenfeld, country house of the Reich Chancellor in Berchtesgaden.
The conservatory (sometimes referred to as the winter garden) appears simply yet comfortably, furnished. Close examination of the wicker chair on the right reveals a swastika incorporated into the design just below the armrests, while the cushion on the back of this chair displays the letters 'AH' beneath a partially observed swastika. The steps in the lower left foreground lead back into the room already discussed in postcard number 96.

99. Haus Wachenfeld, country house of the Reich Chancellor in Berchtesgaden.
Here we view the opposite end of the conservatory to that observed in the previous postcard, number 98.
The windows at the end of the room overlooked the drive and the mountain road, while the large window on the left permitted direct access to the main terrace located above the garage.

DER FÜHRER in seinem Heim Haus Wachenfeld

100. The Führer in his home Haus Wachenfeld.
Hitler pictured in the conservatory at Haus Wachenfeld with his German shepherd, Blondi, a gift to the Führer from Martin Bormann. Hitler adored the dog and delighted in having her perform tricks for friends and guests when gathered on the Obersalzberg. On the morning of 30 April, 1945, on Hitler's orders, the animal was destroyed by means of poison. Later that same day her master took his own life. The reverse of this postcard bears a commemorative postmark stating; *Berlin: 20 April 1937: Des Führers Geburtstag,* (The Führer's Birthday).

Section Two

Berghof: Secondary Seat
of Government

❖

The Führer
and the Surrounding Area

❖

The Munich Agreement

Berghof: Secondary Seat of Government

By the mid 1930s, Hitler's modest alpine cottage, Haus Wachenfeld, was increasingly viewed as a home no longer befitting the German Chancellor; it simply did not reflect Hitler's status. The new 'Berghof' which emerged from the 1935/36 rebuilding programme, having absorbed its humble predecessor, offered the Führer a country residence worthy of his position. When not in Berlin, it was at the Berghof that foreign leaders were received and entertained and later, where important decisions relating to the conduct of the war would be taken.

Hitler, always something of a frustrated architect, drew up his own detailed plans for the Berghof; these were then presented to the well-known Munich architect Alois Degano, who in turn was responsible for overseeing the construction of the new residence. The Führer had shown concern that the building might not be complementary to the landscape due to its size. However, on seeing the completed Berghof he expressed total satisfaction with the entire undertaking.

Berghof Wachenfeld
unseres Führers Heim
inmitten seiner Berchtesgadener Berge

101. Berghof Wachenfeld, the Führer's home in the middle of his Berchtesgaden Mountains.
The term 'Berghof Wachenfeld' used in this caption might seem confusing, however, during construction of the new residence through 1935/36 and on Hitler's instructions, the new building thereafter generally referred to as the Berghof, was sympathetically constructed around Haus Wachenfeld so as to incorporate and preserve the original house to which the Führer was sentimentally attached. This explanation would account for the term 'Berghof Wachenfeld' being applied to the enlarged residence after 1936.
In this instance the Führer's home is viewed from the lower slopes of the Obersalzberg.
By including the fence and shrubbery in the foreground the photographer has cleverly added a degree of rustic charm to the image.

gliche Besuch auf Obersalzberg

102. The daily visit on Obersalzberg.

It has already been stated (caption number 82) that the general public were largely denied access to the Obersalzberg after 1934. However, this postcard would appear to contest that statement. Here we see the Berghof completed in 1936, with a large number of people moving along the road below the house.

We can see that the original gates to the property together with the perimeter fence along the roadside have been removed. This would indicate that security and access points to the area were located elsewhere and more strictly controlled. Consequently, we must assume that this image depicts one of the many 'officially' organized visits to the Obersalzberg for large groups, following the reconstruction. While there are figures on the balcony overlooking the road, identification of these individuals is quite impossible.

103. The Führer on his walk (In the background Berghof Wachenfeld in front of the Hoher Göll).

It is well documented that Hitler enjoyed long walks on the Obersalzberg. It is said he walked at such a pace that others had trouble keeping up with him at times. The adoration enjoyed by Hitler in these early years was the envy of many political leaders worldwide. He had redressed much of the unfair Versailles Treaty which had been forced upon Germany in 1918; huge unemployment and massive inflation had also been tackled successfully. All this, together with the restoration of the armed forces, gave every German the feeling that their nation had regained its place on the world stage. With these achievements in mind, the suggestion has been put forward that, had Adolf Hitler died in mid 1939, he would almost certainly have claimed his place in history as the greatest German statesman who had ever lived – there's food for thought!

Der FÜHRER auf einem Spaziergang (im Hintergrund Berghof Wachenfeld vor dem Hohen Göll)

104. House of the Führer after the 1936 rebuilding.

The impressive new Berghof. However, as with its predecessor Haus Wachenfeld, the Berghof was destined to undergo a number of alterations during its relatively short lifetime. There is a degree of starkness about this image suggesting the possibility that work on the new building had just recently ended. The figures by the roadside appear locked in conversation on the merits of the new residence.

105. Konrad Henlein with the Führer on the Obersalzberg.

Hitler photographed with Konrad Henlein who visited the Berghof in May, 1938, during the Czech crisis. Born on 6 May, 1898, at Maffersdorf in Bohemia, Henlein founded the *Sudeten Deutsche Partei* (Sudeten German Party) towards the end of 1933. This organization received substantial secret funding from the Nazis and went on to become the strongest political party in Czechoslovakia. Henlein contrived to see the Sudetenland, that part of Czechoslovakia bordering Germany and home to a large number of ethnic Germans, joined to the Reich.

Following the conclusion of the Munich Agreement on 30 September, 1938, Henlein was appointed *Reichskommissar* (Reichs Commissioner) for the Sudetenland. On 1 May, 1939, following German occupation of the entire country he became *Reichsstatthalter* (Reichs Governor) of Czechoslovakia with control over civil administration. Captured by the Americans at the end of the Second World War, Konrad Henlein committed suicide on 10 May, 1945, while in detention.

106. Haus Wachenfeld, Obersalzberg.

It is difficult to fault Hitler's choice of location for his mountain residence; the Obersalzberg is itself some of nature's finest handiwork. The whole area is surrounded by rugged mountain peaks that rise from wooded uplands with lush pasture and fast flowing rivers that race to the valley where the nearby town of Berchtesgaden is located. With all this in mind and, given the proximity to his native Austria, it is not difficult to see why Hitler was drawn back to this place time and time again.

107. The home of our Führer on Obersalzberg.

The steep slope in front of the property rises up towards the garage where minor finishing work is being carried out, then on towards the main house where the area around the large picture window remains unfinished and unpainted. While an unidentified man stands on the terrace, the perimeter fence running along the roadside is clearly visible in the foreground.

108. The Führer and Dr Goebbels at Berghof Wachenfeld.

Hitler and Goebbels discuss some topic as they and three comrades stroll away from the house, their progress closely observed by a small group on the terrace. Hitler often walked the relatively short distance to his private teahouse at Mooslahnerkopf with friends in the afternoon; perhaps this was one such occasion. Today the teahouse is nothing more than a ruin, but the view towards Salzburg and its castle, visible from the small clearing close to the site, was something Hitler found inspirational.

109. The Berghof, Obersalzberg.

This was the view from the upper balcony of the Berghof looking towards Berchtesgaden.
The photographer has positioned himself in the middle arch on the second floor balcony, a point we can easily locate in postcard number 107. Here, the attention to detail, even to the roof timbers, can be fully appreciated. The small building in the centre foreground was the last sentry house to be passed on the road before entering the heart of the Nazi complex on the Obersalzberg.

81

110. The Führer's home on Obersalzberg.

The Berghof assumes a more rural appearance in this particular postcard chiefly due to the row of haystacks standing in the right foreground. It is probably safe to say that this photograph of the Führer's mountain home was taken soon after the 1935/36 remodelling programme ended, given the early stage of growth of the line of small trees planted along the roadside behind the haystacks.

111. The Führer's home on Obersalzberg with Watzmann.

An altogether more pleasing study of the Berghof than the previous image, here the growth of established trees and shrubs around the property contribute greatly to the overall look of the residence. An unidentified man stands on the terrace observing the photographer. Whilst obviously in the height of summer the Watzmann in the background retains snow on its uppermost peaks.

112. Uncaptioned.

A thoughtful, reticent Hitler sits on the perimeter wall of the terrace at the Berghof.

This postcard bears a special postmark celebrating the *Werbeschau der KdF Sammlergruppe* (The Commercial Show for the 'Strength through Joy' organization) in Hanover in April, 1941. The 'KdF' (*Kraft durch Freude*) was a recreational organization set up in 1933 as a means to encourage better morale and productivity amongst German workers through various incentive schemes.

113. The Berghof on Obersalzberg.

Comparing this image with postcard number 107, we see that new shutters have been added to the windows of Hitler's study located behind the balcony on the first floor. The large picture window of the Great Hall can be seen below the balcony, if partially obscured by the garage. When required this window could be lowered into the basement by means of a hydraulic system. The smaller part of the building observed on the right and behind the garage is part of the original Haus Wachenfeld which, on Hitler's instructions, had been cleverly incorporated into the new and much larger building in 1935/36.

114. A cheerful fellow hiker with the Führer on the Obersalzberg.

At first glance this image appears to record a spontaneous, unexpected chance meeting between Hitler and an unknown hiker on the Obersalzberg. The stone wall appearing in the background of this photograph would indicate the location as being by the roadside directly below the Berghof. To have been permitted to wander around the Obersalzberg in the mid 1930s, let alone close to the Berghof and accidentally encounter the Führer on the road would have been impossible. The SS man behind Hitler holds an unidentified object in a way as if waiting for the Führer to present it to the young man with whom Hitler is speaking; the evidence tends to indicate a contrived image.

115. Berghof Wachenfeld.

This image, along with postcards numbers 116 and 117, concentrates on that side of the main building which cannot be seen from the drive. Here we get a good view of the main terrace located directly in front of the conservatory. The terrace is clearly provided with more than ample furniture for everyday requirements. A much smaller secondary terrace sits in the foreground. This image, if compared with postcard number 53 (photographed from a similar position) gives an idea of the scale of transformation from early Haus Wachenfeld to Berghof.

116. The Berghof.
This photograph has been taken from a point on the main terrace looking back across the secondary terrace and lawn. In the background we see additional living quarters which were located to the right hand side of the main residence.

117. Haus Wachenfeld (new building).
These steps lead up from the sloping grounds found directly in front of the Führer's residence; again the main terrace which stood above the garage is located immediately behind the wall seen on the left. The tree covered slopes of the Obersalzberg continue up behind the property.

118. Dr Goebbels family visit on Obersalzberg.

The scene is one of informal cordiality. Frau Magda Goebbels (seated far left) together with her husband and two of their children pay a visit to the Berghof. All are amused by the action between the older of the two children and other lady who, although not positively identified may be Christa Schröder, Hitler's long-term secretary. In any case she is certainly a person of some status to have been included in such select company.

119. The Berghof (Haus Wachenfeld), Obersalzberg.

Hitler's country retreat in all its glory. The Berghof was not often photographed in this way, that is to say in a manner that includes the entire structure and the towering background. As we can see, the residence stretched out on both sides from the main part of the house to quite an extent. In this instance the photographer has cleverly given us an image that should, given the subject matter, conform to the usual formalities of a 'landscape' shape in 'portrait' form. In doing so he has captured the beautiful alpine scenery behind the house to best advantage and crowned it with the awe inspiring, dominating Hoher Göll.

120. Obersalzberg. The home of the Führer.

The new Berghof photographed from almost the same point as we have seen Haus Wachenfeld photographed in postcard number 58. In comparing these two images we can determine that both buildings occupy the same site. However, as far as scale, comfort and prestige are concerned they were worlds apart. Haus Wachenfeld, to all intents and purposes, has disappeared having been absorbed into the new building. That point where the drive joins the road is clearly visible.

121. Prime Minister Chamberlain on the Obersalzberg.

Photographed at the Berghof we see left to right; Joachim von Ribbentrop (1893-1946), German Foreign Minister; Neville Chamberlain (1869-1940), British Prime Minister and Adolf Hitler. Behind Hitler stands Dr Paul Schmidt (1899-1970), Hitler's personal interpreter between 1935 and 1945. This rare postcard records Chamberlain's only visit to the Führer's home on the Obersalzberg on 15/16 September, 1938. It was the first time the British Premier had travelled by aeroplane; he had made the journey to meet Hitler in an attempt to solve the Czech crisis which, on the face of it, he had appeared to do. In reality he had merely delayed the inevitable.

122. Obersalzberg.
The home of the Führer.

A fine view of the Führer's country retreat as photographed from the roadside prior to the final alterations to the building. The retaining stone wall which ran the entire length of the upper side of the drive is clearly visible; the identical wall in the foreground is situated by the roadside where it remains today.

123. The Führer greets his visitor.

Having taken up a position where the drive joins the road, a smiling Hitler raises his arm in salute.
Uncharacteristically, this particular postcard gives the impression of a completely contrived image produced purely for propaganda purposes.
The reverse bears a special postmark to celebrate the *Anschluss* (joining) of Austria to the Reich on 10 April, 1938. For Hitler this was a time filled with emotion and a great personal triumph as his homeland became part of the German Reich.

Berghof Wachenfeld mit Watzmann und Hochkalter

124. Berghof Wachenfeld with Watzmann and Hochkalter.
In this instance the photographer has taken up a position near Bormann's house which overlooked Hotel zum Türken (centre) and the Berghof (right). In comparing this image with postcard number 50 we can judge the extent to which both properties have been modernized. On the left are temporary accommodation huts for those working on other buildings situated still further left and out of view; on completion of the work these huts were removed.

125. View from Lockstein towards Salzburg with Führer house.
This distinctive postcard presents the Berghof and the surrounding countryside from an unusual angle. In the lower foreground we see part of the Gutshof, built in 1938 as a farm to produce food for the complex. Just above that is Villa Bechstein, which became accommodation for visiting VIPs including Goebbels, Hess and Mussolini. Above Villa Bechstein and to the left stands Landhaus (country house) Bormann, formerly the home of Dr Richard Seitz. In the centre we see Hotel zum Türken. Right of that is the Berghof while a little higher, and on the extreme right, stands the Georg Arnhold holiday home, also known as 'Klubheim'; after 1935 the 'Gästehaus Hoher Göll', Party guesthouse. Directly below that is the Gutshof *Wirtschaftsgebäude* (economics building).

126. The Führer in front of his home in Berchtesgaden.
Hitler stands on the wall by the perimeter fence in front of the Berghof. The building on the hill-side in the background is Hotel zum Türken. Omnipresent SS men mingle with the smiling crowd who file past, saluting their Führer. On the left and situated opposite the drive to the property is what appears to be a sentry box.

127. Berghof Obersalzberg.
An excellent overall view of the Berghof, in this instance the large picture window of the Great Hall is shown part open. That part of the building seen above and behind the stone built garage is part of the original house, revealing how 'old' and 'new' were cleverly incorporated into one structure. This photograph depicts the Berghof prior to the final rebuilding of the annex on the left, and the construction of a service road in that area as a means of keeping delivery vehicles off the main drive. Bearing a postmark dated; 16.1.41, three weeks later, on 6 February, 1941, Hitler would give command of the newly created *Afrika Korps* to General Erwin Rommel, 'The Desert Fox'.

"Wachenfeld" am Obersalzberg (1000 m) gegen Reiteralpe · 1023·Phot

128. Haus Wachenfeld on Obersalzberg (1,000m) towards Reiteralpe.

This image confirms the activity of continually carrying out alterations of varying scale around the Berghof. Building materials can be seen by the annex door in the foreground and again on the drive at the foot of the main steps. It is difficult to understand why, when having just completed a building which was enormous compared with the original cottage it should be deemed necessary to enlarge the property further still.

129. The home of the Führer on Obersalzberg with Reiteralpe.

In comparison with the previous postcard number 128, it is obvious that the annex in the foreground has been completely rebuilt and enlarged. It stretches out further than previously from the main building and joins a newly constructed service road. Another floor has been added complete with balcony, new shutters have been fitted to all windows and access to the back of the house has been improved with increased space between the building and the hillside. This is basically how the Berghof would remain until its destruction in 1945.

130. Berghof – Obersalzberg near Berchtesgaden.

Here (although very similar to postcard number 129), we can see how the new service road to the enlarged annex joined the mountain road, while vehicles stand on the original drive near the main entrance. The new service road permitted deliveries to the residence without the risk of disturbing the Führer, or his guests; a possibility when the property had been accessed by a single drive. With many high-level meetings being held at the Berghof, such disturbances would not have been welcomed.

131. Photographed in 2004 are the remains of the service road observed in the previous postcard number 130. On reaching the trees at the end of the service road one still finds the retaining wall which was built next to the hillside at the rear of the Berghof, clearly visible in postcard number 129. The site is now very overgrown. However, using the retaining wall together with the remains of the garage a little further along, the determined individual can still work out where the Berghof was located on the site.

132. Photographed in 2004, this is how the aforementioned service road appears when observed form the former site of the Berghof itself; everything is now very overgrown as nature takes over where man left off. The eternal Hotel zum Türken, having miraculously survived, stands on the hillside a little further up the mountain road.

133. Photographed in 2004 we observe the now almost unrecognizable main drive to the Berghof, this led to the steps below the main entrance to the residence and is located a short distance down the road from the previously discussed service road to the property. The only tangible evidence in this instance is the remains of the original stone built wall next to the hillside on the left; this is clearly visible in postcard number 122.

134. Obersalzberg, summer 1937.
Girls from Braunau visit the Führer.
These two young ladies in traditional dress have travelled from Hitler's birthplace Braunau am Inn to meet the Führer at his country home. The SS man on the right is a member of the Führer's personal bodyguard, the *Leibstandarte – SS Adolf Hitler* as indicated on the cuff title of his uniform.

135. The Berghof.
This image sees the Berghof bathed in autumn sunshine as the surrounding trees cast long shadows across the building. The town of Berchtesgaden itself lies hidden under a blanket of thick cloud in the valley below while the Reiteraple in the background display the first signs of approaching winter. Posted on the Obersalzberg and bearing a postmark dated 6.10.42, it was around this time that things began to go badly for German forces on the Eastern front.

136. The Berghof Obersalzberg, entrance.
The main entrance to the residence as viewed from just inside the door. Beyond the arches on the right was a paved area which in turn led to the flight of steps leading down to the drive. If, as was usual upon arrival at the Berghof, the Führer came out to greet his guest, the individual concerned could easily establish their status in the eyes of the Führer. Should Hitler descend to greet them at the bottom of the steps, they were held in some esteem; if on the other hand he waited at the top of the steps for the visitor to reach him, they were not so highly regarded.

Postcard numbers 137 to 143 offer an all round view of the Great Hall (also known as the conference room) at the Berghof. This most impressive room was where the Führer entertained foreign leaders, chosen guests and those members of his inner social circle; during the war years it was a venue for important meetings with his military advisors. For the purposes of maintaining a logical sequence through these images depicting the Great Hall, we will move left to right around the room beginning with postcard number 137.

137. The Berghof Obersalzberg. Part view of the Great Hall.
Many whose names have now been consigned to the history books, were led into the Great Hall through this door. Only the finest quality materials were used in the construction of the Berghof, the marble steps led towards the famous picture window at the opposite end of the room.

138. The Berghof Obersalzberg, Great Hall.
Here we view the seating area around the fine marble fireplace. Hitler, whilst usually seated in one of the chairs in the foreground to the right of the fireplace, would talk long into the early hours with those closest to him. Many and most subjects were discussed during these late night gatherings, but inevitably at some point the conversation always turned to politics.

139. The Berghof Obersalzberg, Great Hall.
Moving back the photographer has taken in more of the room on either side of the fireplace; in doing so this also allows an opportunity to observe the wonderful coffer ceiling.

140. The Berghof Obersalzberg, Great Hall.

The Great Hall as observed from a point close to the picture window. It was in these sumptuous surroundings that many foreign leaders were entertained and flattered by Hitler and, here again, where many were intimidated and subjugated.

141. The Berghof Obersalzberg, Great Hall.

Continuing around the room we arrive near the large conference table situated before the famous window at the opposite end of the room to the fireplace. The saying 'time flies' takes on a different meaning on examining the clock opposite, adorned as it is with the Nazi eagle. The adjoining room, observed through the doorway on the left, is part of the original Haus Wachenfeld; very few images show the internal connections between old and new.

142. Berghof Wachenfeld, view of the Untersberg from the Great Hall.

An excellent view of the large picture window of the Great Hall through which the snow covered Untersberg can be seen across the valley. Standing before this window Adolf Hitler could see his native Austria in the distance. Interestingly, this caption refers to the residence as 'Berghof Wachenfeld', a situation brought about by the act of physically incorporating the original Haus Wachenfeld into the new building, the Berghof.

143. The Berghof Obersalzberg, Great Hall.

The Great Hall, with fabulous tapestries hung around the walls, was tastefully and comfortably furnished. This seating area was located to the right of the large picture window. While the Berghof had been decorated and furnished to a very high standard there was nothing ostentatious about what had been achieved.

144. The Berghof Obersalzberg, living room.

This cosy living room, originally part of Haus Wachenfeld, was adjacent to the Great Hall. We can see the connecting doorway between the two rooms in postcard number 141. The large structure on the extreme left, covered in ceramic tiles, is in fact a wood burning stove; these remain a popular and practical form of heating and traditionally continue to exist in many German properties today.

145. The Berghof Obersalzberg, guest room.

If, as stated in the caption on the reverse, we accept this photograph as representing typical guest accommodation at the Berghof, the image goes some way in dispelling any preconceptions of opulent living at Hitler's country residence. The overall impression is one of simple homely comfort.

146. The Berghof Obersalzberg, winter garden.
This study of the winter garden at the newly constructed Berghof shows it to be quite different from its predecessor at Haus Wachenfeld (observed in postcards numbers 98 and 99). The large window on the left looked out across the valley towards the Untersberg while also permitting direct access to the main terrace located above the garage.

147. The Berghof Obersalzberg, winter garden.
This image shows the opposite end of the conservatory which overlooked the secondary terrace already observed in postcard number 115. Again, as with other rooms in the residence where there was no great need for formality, other than obviously the Great Hall, furnishings are richly patterned and inviting.

148. The Berghof Obersalzberg, dining room.

This is the dining room used by Hitler and his guests. Rare and expensive cembra pine has been used as wall panelling, in today's terms it would cost a vast amount to install. The Führer, a strict vegetarian after 1931 did not smoke, nor did he like alcohol; on occasion he might sip a glass of champagne but generally preferred to indulge a liking for herbal drinks.

149. The Berghof Obersalzberg, dining room.

Another view of the Führer's dining room, this time photographed from the opposite side to that seen in the previous postcard number 148; this image reveals the area of the bay window and the furniture contained there. In general terms there appears to have been nothing ostentatious about the Berghof in any real sense.

150. The Berghof Obersalzberg, guest room.
This particular postcard has been encountered with a caption stating it to be Eva Braun's room; however in most instances it is simply described as a guest room. Whatever the case, it provided every comfort for a pleasant stay.

151. Berghof Wachenfeld, study of the Führer.
A splendid view of Hitler's study situated on the first floor above the Great Hall. The large windows opened onto a long balcony (seen clearly in postcard number 111) allowing the Führer privacy to enjoy the fabulous uninterrupted views across the valley. Hitler's desk is located before the middle window; the portrait hanging to the left of this window is certainly Hitler's mother, while the other, to the right of the desk and partially obscured by the lamp, appears to be of his father.

152. Berghof Wachenfeld, study of the Führer.

Here we observe that part of the study opposite the windows. The Führer's desk is on the left; the fitted bookcases at the other end of the room appear well filled and probably include a copy of *Mein Kampf*. The mood of the study is one of intimacy and stylish comfort. This particular postcard bears an Obersalzberg postmark dated 1.7.37 from where it has made its way to an address in Münster.

153. The Führer in his study on Obersalzberg.

Hitler, wearing a light coloured double-breasted suit looks solemnly towards the camera while seated at his desk in the Berghof. Hoffmann, the Führer's photographer, has obviously managed to persuade Hitler to sit at his desk purely to make this image more interesting and complete; the total lack of paperwork on the desk makes this abundantly clear.

The Führer and the Surrounding Area

The following postcards, numbers 154 to 179, observe Hitler both on the Obersalzberg and in the surrounding area. The Führer is depicted in numerous situations, whether in the company of associates, alone or interacting with some of the nameless thousands who descended on the region in the hope of encountering him. Each of these had their own reasons for making the journey, sometimes hundreds of miles; motives ranging from total devotion to simple curiosity.

154. The Führer with his most loyal supporters in Bad Elster, 22 June, 1930.
Included in this small group of leading Nazis are, from left to right; Heinrich Himmler (1900-45), head of the SS and chief of Gestapo. Behind Himmler stands Martin Mutschmann, Gauleiter of Saxony. The man at the rear in the doorway remains unidentified. Beside Himmler stands Dr Wilhelm Frick (1877-1946), Reich Minister for the Interior. Adolf Hitler. Immediately behind Hitler stands Dr Paul Joseph Goebbels (1897-1945), Minister for Propaganda. Julius Schaub, adjutant to Hitler. General Franz Ritter von Epp (1868-1947), Governor of Bavaria and Reich Leader of the NSDAP. On the extreme right stands Hermann Wilhelm Goering (1893-1946), chief of the Luftwaffe and Reich President. Bad Elster is a small town situated in southern Saxony close to the Czech border. This photograph was probably taken at the time of the provincial elections held in the region in June, 1930, which resulted in the Nazis becoming the second strongest party in Saxony. Such early images depicting the main Nazi leadership together in this way, are quite rare.

105

er kleine Autogrammjäger

155. The little autograph hunter.

A young admirer requests the Führer's autograph. As Hitler prepares to sign the ubiquitous postcard which was customary on such occasions, he appears to observe the lad with some affection; the boy's attention however remains fixed on the postcard itself. This endearing scene depicts the approachable and caring leader who gives of himself without hesitation.

156. The Führer in the Predigtstuhl Mountain Hotel near Berchtesgaden.

Hitler relaxes on the terrace at the Predigtstuhl Hotel which is located on the mountain of the same name near Bad Reichenhall, a short distance from Berchtesgaden. Access to the hotel is via the famous *Predigtstuhl Bahn* (cable car), the first in Germany. It opened on 1 July, 1928, and takes less than ten minutes to reach the hotel situated at a height of 1,583 metres. The views over Bad Reichenhall and the surrounding area from the hotel terrace are breathtaking. The building was used by the US after 1945 but has since been returned to German hands.

157. The little autograph hunter.

A caring Hitler shares an intimate moment with a proud mother and her daughter who has been fortunate enough to receive the Führer's autograph, something she will always remember. This encounter, as with the previous postcard number 156, has been photographed on the occasion of Hitler's visit to the Predigtstuhl Hotel.

158. The Reich Chancellor Adolf Hitler in his beloved mountains.

While out on one of his numerous walks in the area Hitler stops to talk to this small boy. In the background is Geli Raubal, the daughter of Hitler's half-sister Angela, his housekeeper at Haus Wachenfeld. Geli committed suicide in Hitler's Munich flat (while Hitler himself was travelling to Hamburg for a meeting with SA leaders) on the night of 17/18 September, 1931, amid rumours of their having had an affair, though this has never been proved. Following the untimely death of his niece, Hitler remained inconsolable for many weeks.

159. The People's Chancellor, Adolf Hitler, in Berchtesgaden.

The Führer, having just been presented with flowers by this local girl passes them rather smartly to his SA adjutant, Wilhelm Brückner; the young lady meanwhile appears somewhat awe stricken by the whole experience. This postcard bears a postmark dated 26.8.34; Hitler had recently declared himself 'Head of the German State' following the death, on 2 August, of President von Hindenburg (1847-1934).

160. Her wish is fulfilled.

A young lady, who bears a striking resemblance to the girl seen in the previous postcard number 159, poses with the Führer. She carries a postcard of Hitler which will be duly autographed. At the time this was equivalent to being photographed with your favourite film or pop star, such was the popularity and adoration enjoyed by Hitler; true celebrity status.

161. A quiet hour in the Berchtesgaden area.
Hitler poses thoughtfully for the camera amid tranquil surroundings near Berchtesgaden. The postmark on the reverse states; *München 19.10.38 Hauptstadt der Bewegung* (Capital of the Movement), Munich is thus celebrated as the foundation city of the NSDAP.

162. A Berchtesgaden boy greets the Führer.
Members of the SA and SS accompany the Führer on walkabout as he is greeted by a local child selected from the crowd. As a smiling Hitler takes the boy's hand the photographer captures a vote winning image that sets the standard for modern political campaigning. While photographed in the early 1930s, this image is proof of the direct relationship between early Nazi campaigning methods and modern electioneering techniques that have been adopted directly from Nazi innovation. The Nazis pioneered many of today's basic electioneering principles; advanced ideas that are still used very successfully by numerous politicians worldwide.

chtesgadener Bua begrüßt den Führer.

im Hintersee bei Berchtesgaden

163. The Führer at Hintersee near Berchtesgaden.

Yet another charming image from the continuing programme for the winning of hearts and minds. Hitler chats with two local children while visiting the Hintersee located near Ramsau, not far from Berchtesgaden. Following an unbelievable stroke of luck, and by sheer coincidence, I discovered that the small boy seen photographed with Hitler, still lived in the region. Here was an opportunity not to be missed; having acquired a telephone number I made contact with this gentleman and, having explained my interest he kindly agreed to a meeting later that same week.

The bus journey from Berchtesgaden to Hintersee takes about forty-five minutes, passing through some of the most wonderful alpine scenery on the way. On arrival at Hintersee, I made my way to 'Bartels Alpenhof', the address I had been given for our two o'clock meeting. Bartels Alpenhof is a long established family business where, on making enquiries I was led to the large kitchen where I was introduced to the subject of my attention. Gerhard Bartels, now over seventy years old, is a charming man who continues to work in the hotel as he has done for over sixty years. We spent the next hour talking in a quiet part of the hotel where Gerhard, who gave generously of his time, recalled what he remembered from the occasion of being photographed with Hitler in the summer of 1937.

Born in January, 1932, Gerhard clearly remembers being told on the day that he must wear clean clothes, he must not get dirty, he was being photographed. 'I was not allowed to play with the others; I might get my clothes dirty' recalls Gerhard, 'I didn't like that, I just wanted to be out with the other children.' At the time he could not understand what all the fuss was about.

The little girl who appears in the photograph was Gerhard's cousin, Anni, born in July, 1931, (Anni, unfortunately, is no longer alive). Anni's father, Dori Weiss, (Gerhard's uncle) had been Hitler's sergeant for a time during the First World War. The two men subsequently kept in contact, with Hitler visiting his old comrade at the Hintersee almost every summer. Dori Weiss, who died in 1941, was the proprietor of the nearby 'Hotel Post', the location for the photographic session. The former hotel now operates as a youth hostel and is situated approximately 300 metres from Bartels Alpenhof.

It was through this personal contact that Gerhard and Anni were selected to be photographed with the Führer on that occasion. During the photographic session Gerhard remembers Hitler asked, 'What kind of cake do you like to eat?' Gerhard replied 'Apple cake'. At the end of the session, Gerhard, when finally released from all restrictions and running off to play was asked; 'What did the Führer say to you?' To which he replied 'I don't remember; it wasn't important!' During the course of our conversation it emerged that the apple cake in question has yet to materialize.

Bartels Alpenhof overlooks the Hintersee beyond which stands the magnificent Watzmann. Following the bombing of the Obersalzberg on 25 April, 1945 and, on Hitler's orders, the building was taken over by Albert Bormann, Martin Bormann's brother. Many former employees of the Berghof together with numerous SS officers and Hitler's private secretary, Christa Schröder, then began living at Alpenhof. The hotel had in effect become the last headquarters of the Third Reich. With the arrival of the Americans in the area on 8 May, 1945, the men recently arrived from the Berghof then made every attempt to evade capture by fleeing into the surrounding countryside.

Gerhard clearly remembers seeing Hitler's fabulous Mercedes 770 motor car parked in the barn behind the house after the war; strangely the vehicle disappeared soon after, only to miraculously reappear in America sometime later. To have unexpectedly located Gerhard Bartels during my last trip to the region prior to publication, was remarkable; it is best described one of those experiences that defy explanation. For having agreed to see me, for his hospitality and for being so generous in both time and memories, I remain most grateful.

164. Uncaptioned.
Whether Hitler's decision or that of the photographer, an attempt is made to get just one more photograph with the still immaculately dressed Gerhard Bartels who appears in postcard number 163. However it is plainly obvious that young Gerhard has had quite enough; he draws away from the Führer, who in turn keeps hold of the boy lest he run off. Consequently, and with this in mind, it is difficult to understand why an image which clearly fails in its objective to depict the warm interaction between Hitler and the young was ever passed for publication. We can safely assume that this would have been the last photograph taken of Hitler and little Gerhard on the day; further attempts would have necessitated tying the youngster to a chair to keep him from his playmates.

165. German Youth greet the Führer.
While displaying great discipline by standing to attention and patiently awaiting the Führer's greeting, the older boys cannot hide the excitement on their faces; Hitler meanwhile, engages the smallest of this little group of ardent followers. This photograph was taken on the same occasion as postcards numbers 163 and 164, this can be determined in two ways; firstly, Hitler is seen wearing the same suit in all cases; secondly, the building in the background together with the furniture seen in postcards numbers 163 and 165 are one and the same.

166. Guests by the fence on Obersalzberg.
His people have come to the Obersalzberg and their Führer has not disappointed them. The photographer has chosen his moment well, the delight and excitement on the faces in the crowd is almost contagious and, just as Hitler picks out this young girl for particular attention the camera captures an image full of the 'ah' factor. Photographs depicting a political leader endearing himself to the people don't come any better.

chskanzler Hitler bei einem Morgenausflug
in seinem Berchtesgadener Land

Phot. H.

167. Reich Chancellor Hitler on his morning outing in his Berchtesgaden land.

Everything about this image suggests the group to be unaware of the photographer's presence. Close examination of this postcard reveals it to be a montage, where the group sitting around the table have been placed into what we must assume to be a more interesting background than that of the original photograph. German photographers were particularly adept in such techniques, so much so that it is sometimes difficult to detect.

The background itself would suggest the location to be Mooslahnerkopf, below Haus Wachenfeld where Bormann would build Hitler's teahouse in 1937. The reverse bears a postmark dated 5.10.33, part of the postmark then promotes; *Skimeisterschaft der Deutschen: 8-12 Februar 1934 : Berchtesgaden : Bayerische Alpen*, the German Skiing Championships to be held in Berchtesgaden in February, 1934.

erzlichen Dank

168. A hearty thanks.

Hitler looks affectionately at the little girl he knows so well; she has already appeared in postcards numbers 45, 71, 89 and 90. Here she is seen accepting gifts from the Führer while the crowds file past in the background. Hitler must have felt genuine affection for this particular child given that she was photographed with him on so many occasions.

169. Hitler with the youth in the mountains.

Here the Führer is depicted as the personal friend and guardian of young people. As time passed, countless thousands of young people came to believe in Hitler as that personal friend and father figure through the encouragement of the many youth organizations set up for that very purpose.

170. Berchtesgaden children congratulate the Führer.
This unidentified event sees Hitler giving apples to the girl closest to the camera. These two girls, together with the almost completely obscured younger boy on Hitler's left are the same children to appear in the previous postcard number 169. It is reasonable to assume that these photographs, together with the next image number 171, were all taken on the same occasion, as part of an exercise depicting the Führer interacting with young people.

71. Visit on the Obersalzberg.
With Hitler in attendance, two of the children already observed in postcards numbers 169 and 170 are presented with gifts by Magda and Joseph Goebbels as their visit to the Obersalzberg comes to an end.

Such images have but one purpose; to promote the Führer, and in this instance other members of the Nazi hierarchy, as caring and approachable while appearing genuinely interested in young people.

172. A little one's visit.
While enjoying some refreshment the Führer graciously receives a littl[e] girl who is obviously another autograph hunte[r] Hitler appears to hold th[e] ubiquitous postcard in a way so as to tease the ch[ild] nonetheless, she will receive her memento, du[ly] signed, before returning [to] her family who are prob[ably] just out of camera shot.

173. Reich Chancellor Adolf Hitler and Reich Youth Leader Baldur von Schirach.
Hitler, appearing confident and composed, now carries the aura of authority with ease. He is a man who welcomes and understands the adoration of his people and their need of him. Standing behind Hitler is Baldur von Schirach, the man responsible for the education of German youth in the ways of National Socialism; he sows the seed that will flower in obedience to the Führer's will.

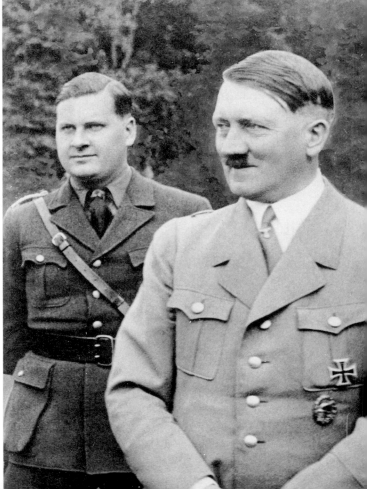

Der FÜHRER auf dem Königs[e]

174. The Führer on the Königssee.

The beautiful Königsee, always a popular tourist attraction. Here Hitler sits in the stern of what is probably a pleasure craft. These boats are electrically powered so as to eliminate the risk of pollution to the clear waters of the lake. The Führer's expression and demeanour suggest his mind may be occupied elsewhere.

175. The Führer at Obersee-Königssee.

To reach the spot where Hitler is observed in this postcard is a journey of approximately one and a half hours from Berchtesgaden. The bus trip from Berchtesgaden (Train Station) to the Königssee takes just under fifteen minutes. The boat trip to Salletalm at the opposite end of the lake itself takes about fifty minutes, leaving a fifteen minute walk along the path to the Obersee. On reaching the Obersee one finds the instantly recognizable large rock before which the Führer is standing. With scenery that is undoubtedly some of the best in the region this trip is well worth the effort.

Unser Führer am Obersee-Königssee

176. Photographed in 2004 is the location observed in the previous postcard, number 175. While the water level of the Obersee is currently higher than at the time when Hitler was photographed at the same spot in the mid 1930s, and while there are more trees in the immediate area, this is unmistakably the same distinctive rock by the water's edge.

177. The Chancellor at the Obersee near Berchtesgaden.

A wistful, uniformed Hitler sits on a rock located only a few metres from the spot observed in postcard number 175 during another visit to the Obersee. As with certain other postcards, this image has been encountered where it includes another individual on the rock behind the Führer. However on this occasion, as is most commonly the case, the Führer sits alone.

Der Kanzler am Obers
bei Berchtesgaden

178. Photographed in 2004 is the location observed in the previous postcard number 177. Having spent some time examining the rock formations along the edge of the Obersee and, allowing for the considerable growth of trees in the immediate area during the interim, this particular rock emerges as that most likely used by the Führer as his resting place.

179. With the Führer People's Chancellor Adolf Hitler on the Obersalzberg.

Enthusiastic crowds salute and greet their Führer as he exchanges a few words with a young woman at the front of this orderly line; the SS are never far away all the while maintaining order and protecting the Führer. Posted in Dresden on 28.2.34, this postcard then made its way to an address in Stuttgart carrying birthday greetings; an unusual subject matter for a birthday card!

The Munich Agreement

While perhaps not directly relevant to the subject matter of this book, the Munich Agreement held more importance for Hitler than might be considered at a glance. Firstly, there was the fact that the negotiations were held and concluded in Munich, the city where the Führer's political career as a beer-hall agitator had begun, and almost ended. Secondly, it allowed Hitler to dictate the terms of the agreement to Germany's old adversaries and the dictators of the Versailles Treaty; France and England.

The Munich Agreement was probably the Führer's greatest, single diplomatic success; if a bitter-sweet victory for Hitler on a personal level. Through skilful manipulation of all parties concerned, he had achieved exactly what he had set out to do, and yet, he had been denied the one thing he really wanted – the military conquest of Czechoslovakia.

The following postcards are a fascinating visual record of the event which took place in the Führer House (already observed in postcard number 18) in Munich on 29/30 September, 1938. In the final analysis, the Munich Agreement permitted German forces unhindered entry and occupation of the Sudetenland in Czechoslovakia; this was carried out peacefully and as scheduled the following day, 1 October, 1938. Hitler had seen the weakness of the French and British for himself during the negotiations in Munich; the results of these observations would soon be felt throughout Europe, and beyond.

180. 29.9.38 Kufstein.
Two statesmen and friends greet each other.
Hitler and Mussolini exchange warm greetings as the Italian leader alights from his train at Kufstein on the Austrian-German border. He was en route to Munich to take part in the negotiations which were essentially the beginning of the end for Czechoslovakia. Hitler boarded the train at Kufstein where the two leaders spent the remainder of the journey in discussions about the meeting scheduled to begin later that afternoon. It was Mussolini who had suggested the four power conference with the intention of reaching peaceful agreement to the Czech crisis, then near breaking point. Again, it was Mussolini who produced the documents suggesting the order of business for the conference. In reality these proposals had been drawn up by the Germans only the day before, but it was believed a better result would be achieved if they were introduced to the meeting by the Italian leader as his own ideas.

181. Uncaptioned.

It is hardly surprising to find this postcard uncaptioned; one must remember it was produced at a time when both men had achieved such eminence on the European political stage that they were considered instantly recognizable. This superb Hoffmann image sees Benito Mussolini, Fascist leader of Italy, standing next his friend and ally Adolf Hitler, Nazi leader of Germany.

The photograph was probably taken at some point during the conference held in the Führer House in Munich in September, 1938, which concluded in the 'Munich Agreement'. Through the latter half of the 1920s Hitler had viewed Mussolini's success in Italy with a mixture of envy and admiration; a decade later, it was Mussolini who stood in awe and admiration of Hitler as the Führer's deeds surpassed his own achievements. Thereafter 'the Duce' (Mussolini) played a subordinate role in a relationship dominated by Hitler.

Benito Mussolini was born at Dovia in the province of Forlì on 29 July, 1883. In 1902, following a short time as a school teacher he travelled to Switzerland where, among other things, he worked as a translator. Returning to Italy in 1905 he spent a year in the army. On Italy's entering the First World War in 1915, Mussolini volunteered and served until wounded during military exercises in 1917. After the war his political views seem to have changed on more than one occasion; having starting out a staunch socialist, Mussolini later embraced the extreme nationalism he would maintain for the rest of his life.

Mussolini and Hitler shared certain similarities, not least of which were the ways both men were to achieve political success. Their appeal to the masses and the methods used to promote their political ideas as a cure for the severe economic crises ravaging their respective countries at the time. Mussolini, as with Hitler in Germany, won the support of a cross section of the population through his oratory and the accompanying ferocious street battles. Having achieved substantial political success in 1921 with over thirty seats in the Italian parliament, Mussolini and his Blackshirts marched on Rome in October, 1922, forcing the resignation of the Italian Premier, Luigi Facta. Within two years the new Italian leader had silenced all opposition.

On 25 July, 1943, following more military setbacks than successes, with the threat of Allied invasion and his support at home disappearing, Mussolini was summoned and dismissed by King Victor Emmanuel. Having endured detention at various locations following his dismissal, Mussolini attempted an escape to Switzerland; the attempt failed when the small group were captured by Italian partisans. Benito Mussolini, his comrades and his mistress Clara Petacci, who was travelling with him, were executed on 28 April, 1945; their bodies were then displayed in a grotesque and most undignified way in a public square in Milan.

The news of Mussolini's death and the gruesome way his body had been put on public display, shocked Hitler. This, as much as any other reason, accounts for the Führer's decision that he would not be captured alive. As the Red Army encircled Berlin in 1945, Hitler feared that his remains, if discovered, might also be put on display; perhaps even in Moscow by his ideological enemy Stalin. The Führer ordered that, in the event of his death, his remains be disposed of by fire. Following his suicide on 30 April, 1945, this order was obediently carried out. SS Major Otto Günsche (Hitler's adjutant) assisted by SS Major Erich Kempka (Hitler's chauffeur) and SS Major Heinz Linge (Hitler's valet) performed this final task together.

182. The Führer and Prime Minister Chamberlain.

Hitler and Chamberlain pose for the photographer. While neither individual looks particularly comfortable, the British Prime Minister, through circumstances chiefly due to his choice in clothes, appears to represent something from a bygone age. A seemingly impassive Hitler assumes a more formal pose.

183. Prime Minister Daladier signs the Munich Agreement.

Édouard Daladier, the French leader, adds his signature to the Agreement which effectively sealed the fate of the independent state of Czechoslovakia. Ribbentrop, (Hitler's Minister for Foreign Affairs) on the extreme right leans on the desk observing the moment while Dr Schmidt, Hitler's interpreter, is seen on the left. Two commemorative Nazi postmarks celebrating the event appear on the reverse of this postcard.

184. Prime Minister Chamberlain signs the Munich Agreement.

Chamberlain carefully adds his signature to the Agreement under the watchful eye of Mussolini, who leans on the chair behind the British Premier. The reverse of this postcard carries a slogan stating; *'Sudetenland durch Adolf Hitler frei, Okt. 1938'* (The Sudetenland is free through Adolf Hitler, Oct. 1938). While the Agreement was concluded on 30 September, it was the following day, 1 October, 1938, that saw German forces cross the Czech border and peacefully occupy the Sudetenland.

185. Head of Government Mussolini signs the Munich Agreement.

The Italian leader adds his signature to the Agreement. Dr Paul Schmidt who had acted as official interpreter throughout the conference observes the moment, blotter in hand.

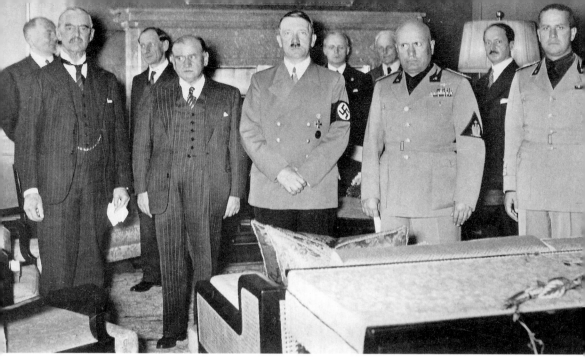

186. Historic four power conference in Munich 29.9.38.
The leaders of the four powers and signatories of the Munich Agreement on 30 September 1938. Standing left to right are Chamberlain (Britain), Daladier (France), Hitler (Germany) and Mussolini (Italy). On the extreme right stands the Italian Foreign Minister, Count Galeazzo Ciano (Mussolini's son-in-law).

187. Visit of Prime Minister Chamberlain to the private residence of the Führer on 30.9.38.
The British Premier visiting the Führer at his Munich flat on the morning of 30 September, 1938, prior to his return to England later that afternoon. During the meeting Chamberlain produced a statement he had drafted advocating that their two countries should never again go to war with one another. Hitler agreed, both leaders added their signatures to the document and Chamberlain then presented Hitler with a copy of their personal agreement. On reaching London later that day the British Prime Minister triumphantly held this same piece of paper aloft announcing; *'Peace for our time'*.

Section Three

The Platterhof Hotel

❖

Goering's Obersalzberg Home

❖

Other Buildings on the
Obersalzberg

❖

The Destruction of the
Obersalzberg

❖

The Kehlsteinhaus (Eagle's Nest)

❖

Nazi Buildings Around
Berchtesgaden

The
Platterhof Hotel

The Platterhof Hotel, originally the 'Steinhauslehen' farm was acquired in 1877 by Mauritia 'Moritz' Mayer. This single-minded, enterprising lady set about turning the property into a guesthouse, renaming it 'Pension Moritz'. This led to a considerable increase in the number of visitors to the area, but it was not until 1888, when the railway arrived in Berchtesgaden that the region was really thrown open to tourism. The area had acquired a reputation as an 'air cure resort' attracting people for the quality of the mountain air and beautiful scenery. The Mayer family continued to run the business until 1917, after which time the property changed hands. In 1919 two doctors from Berlin, Ernst and Eugen Josef, bought the business. In 1921 they installed one Bruno Büchner, a former engineer and pilot to run the guesthouse on a concessionary basis. Büchner and his wife purchased the property in 1923. On making his first visit to the area later that year, Adolf Hitler readily found accommodation at Pension Moritz where he became a regular patron.

Martin Bormann, 'Lord of the Obersalzberg' purchased the guesthouse in 1937 by which time it had already been renamed 'Platterhof'. Between 1939 and 1941 the Platterhof underwent reconstruction on a massive scale, however, once again on Hitler's instructions, as with Haus Wachenfeld the old building was 'incorporated' into the new one, thus preserving as much of the original guesthouse as possible. Boasting absolute luxury the new Platterhof opened on 1 September, 1941. Unfortunately the life of 'Gasthof Platterhof' was to be short-lived. The hotel, having received guests for a mere eighteen months was given over to operate as a military hospital due to the deteriorating war situation and remained as such until the end of the war.

During the bombing of the area in April, 1945, the Platterhof complex suffered considerable damage, particularly the employees' accommodation block; the main hotel itself survived the attack relatively well. Having been restored and renamed 'General Walker Hotel' the complex re-opened in 1953, thereafter serving as a recreational facility for US forces until 1996 when the entire area was returned to the Bavarian State. Amid much controversy the hotel was demolished in 2000. The former site of the Platterhof Hotel is now a car park and bus terminal serving the nearby recently constructed Documentation Centre and, a departure point for buses going on to the Kehlsteinhaus (Eagle's Nest).

Postcard numbers 188 to 191 depict Pension Moritz in the early days when it was still a simple guesthouse offering relaxation amid beautiful surroundings. Postcard numbers 192 to 205 depict the later Platterhof as rebuilt under Martin Bormann's direct influence.

188. Hotel and Guesthouse Moritz, 1,000m. Obersalzberg-Berchtesgaden.

An early view of Pension Moritz prior to any major development of the property. Few postcards show the cowsheds on the right; these were later demolished. The town of Berchtesgaden sits in the valley on the right, the background is provided by the Reiteraple while on the left stand the Hochkalter mountains.

189. Platterhof on the Obersalzberg with Untersberg.

The mighty Untersberg forms the backdrop to this charming alpine scene where the caption clearly indicates the new name of the hotel. On the right above the building stands a flagpole, unusually in this instance topped with a swastika; its very presence implies this image is probably post 1933.

190. Mountain restaurant Platterhof with the Untersberg.

In comparing this image with the pervious postcard, number 189, we can appreciate the changes that have taken place at the Platterhof. There is a degree of starkness about this photograph, brought about by the creation of the open areas around the building where previously there were trees and pasture. Much of the early rustic charm has already been lost through this limited development.

191. Mountain restaurant Platterhof with the Untersberg.

The Platterhof is now in a position to receive visitors arriving by bus, thanks to the large parking area which has been created at the expense of the landscape. With business increased, additional accommodation has been provided in the new building visible through the trees on the extreme right. In the background the Untersberg range stands sprinkled with snow.

192. The Platterhof on the Obersalzberg.
The fabulous new Platterhof Hotel, having cost much more than was originally estimated during its two year construction, opened on 1 September, 1941. Using only the finest quality materials available, the new Platterhof had been conceived as a 'people's hotel' to accommodate the Party faithful. In reality it became a showpiece to accommodate visiting dignitaries.

193. The Platterhof Hotel.
Looking at this image and comparing it with postcard number 189 we can see that the new hotel is located in the same area as the much smaller Platterhof of earlier times. The building furthest away in the background on the left is 'Klubheim', (also clearly visible in postcard number 190) now rebuilt and renamed Gästehaus Hoher Göll; it was used as accommodation by Hitler's Chiefs of Staff and high-ranking Party members visiting the area. Martin Bormann's main office was also located in the building.

194. Photographed in 2004 and from a similar position to that adopted by the photographer of the previous postcard, number 193, the changes in the area appear quite staggering. A large parking area has been created where the hotel complex once stood; the small building on the left is the only thing to link these two images, a last piece of the once fashionable Platterhof to remain standing.

195. Platterhof, terrace view.
The Hochkalter mountains (left) and the Reiteralpe (right) as viewed from the Platterhof terrace. Photographed from a point found in postcard number 19 being just inside the archway located on the extreme left whe the few steps next to the short wall lead t this particular arch.

196. Approach to the Platterhof.

The Reiteralpe provide the background in this instance where the hotel has been photographed from a position opposite to that shown in postcard number 192. The large building on the right is where reception was located.

Guests generally travelled the relatively short distance between the hotel and Berchtesgaden's large and impressive new train station (rebuilt in 1937) by bus.

197. Platterhof towards Reiteralpe.

This photograph has been taken from a position where the photographer has moved much further back in relation to the previous image number 196. Here we view virtually the entire complex from the east. The flagpole, observed here to the left of the main building is a good point of reference to draw comparisons between the two images, appearing as it does in the previous postcard.

198. Platterhof with Watzmann and Hochkalter.

Magnificent alpine scenery forms the backdrop to this fine view of the entire hotel complex. That part of the hotel closest to us was the employees' accommodation block. In this instance the photographer has taken up a position on the hillside near Bormann's house; the rooftops in the foreground are part of the large SS barracks.

199. The Platterhof reception hall.

Reception at the Platterhof was spacious and furnished in traditional Bavarian style; numerous room keys hang behind the main desk while newspapers are provided on the table to the left. The large portrait of Hitler at the opposite end of the room goes almost unnoticed at this distance. Information on the reverse of this postcard reads; The Platterhof Hotel, Obersalzberg above Berchtesgaden. Telephone: Berchtesgaden 2921. Patrons are currently experiencing horrendous problems with the line; with the result that reservations are almost impossible.

200. Large dining room in the Platterhof.
Elegant surroundings with tables set a discreet distance apart. The six large columns supporting the ceiling of the dining room were formed of Untersberg marble. As already stated only the finest quality materials were used in construction; this was reflected throughout the hotel even to the smallest detail.

201. Coffee hall in the Platterhof.
The coffee hall. This particular part of the hotel operated as a completely separate enterprise having been established to provide the visiting Party faithful with refreshment during their 'pilgrimage' to the Führer's home and the Obersalzberg. The hotel logo is visible on the tableware.

202. Coffee hall in the Platterhof.

The coffee hall again. This time we observe the rich tapestries hanging on the wall opposite the windows seen in the previous postcard, number 201. Again the large window frames in the coffee hall were formed of fine Untersberg marble.

203. Platterhof, the Mountain Inn.

The Platterhof's Mountain Inn provided refreshment for those groups visiting the Obersalzberg through the later, officially organized, trips to the region. Following the aforementioned restrictions introduced in 1934 (denying the general public access to the Obersalzberg in the previously uncontrolled huge numbers), these officially sanctioned tours then offered the public virtually their only opportunity to visit the Nazi complex.

204. Platterhof, the Mountain Inn.
The Mountain Inn photographed from a point diagonally opposite to that of the previous image and looking back towards the main entrance.

205. The Platterhof, the Wooden Room.
This particular postcard confirms the level of expenditure lavished on the building. The cembra pine used throughout this room is of the type already discussed in caption number 148, referring to the dining room at the Berghof. To install this particular panelling today would be extremely expensive.

Goering's Obersalzberg Home

The following section, postcard numbers 206 to 218 deals with the country home of Hermann Goering and his family on the Obersalzberg. The Goering home, unlike Hitler's residence nearby was not extensively photographed; consequently postcards depicting Goering's property are limited and quite scarce.

The house itself was situated in the same region of the Obersalzberg as the Bormann family home. That said its location probably offered Goering more privacy than any other resident living inside the central zone. It has been stated that the property occupied one of the most beautiful parts of the Obersalzberg. Hermann Goering, unlike his neighbour Martin Bormann, enjoyed a high level of popularity with the people of Berchtesgaden due to his decent attitude towards them.

Generalfeldmarschall Hermann Göring
mit Gattin und Töchterchen

206. General Field Marshal Hermann Goering with wife and little daughter.
A nicely posed family photograph where Goering and his wife Emmy gaze adoringly at their only child, Edda. Hermann Goering married his second wife, the actress Emmy Sonnemann on 10 April, 1935, amid great ceremony in Berlin; Adolf Hitler acted as best man. Goering's first wife, Carin von Kantzow, the daughter of a Swedish nobleman, died of tuberculosis on 17 October, 1931, leaving her husband devastated.

207. Goering's mountain home on Obersalzberg (1,000m).
While giving the impression of having been photographed surreptitiously, this charming image offers a glimpse of the residence through the branches of nearby evergreens.

208. The christening in the Goering home.
This fabulous image sees proud parents Emmy and Hermann Goering on the occasion of the christening of their little daughter Edda, in 1938. Hitler, at Goering's request, had accepted the role of godfather to the child.

209. Hermann Goering's home on Obersalzberg 1,000m above sea level.

This photograph depicts the Goering home at a stage close to completion. Inspection of the foreground reveals building materials and evidence of minor finishing work still in progress.

210. The General Field Marshal and his little daughter.

Goering the proud father, poses for the camera with his daughter Edda. The child was born in Berlin on 2 June, 1938. In later life Edda followed a career in nursing. Interestingly the reverse of this postcard bears a postmark dated; 10.7.40, the day the *Luftwaffe* began their attacks on England.

211. Hermann Goering house on Obersalzberg.
This image shows the property from the opposite side to that seen in postcard number 209. Taken together they offer a good all round view of the house. The abundance of wild alpine flowers in the foreground contributes greatly to the overall charm of the image.

212. The home of our General Field Marshal Hermann Goering on Obersalzberg.
In this instance Goering's Obersalzberg home is photographed looking towards Salzburg in neighbouring Austria. The property was typically Upper Bavarian in style; its location, although only minutes on foot from the Berghof and the heart of the complex afforded seclusion.

Frau Emmy Göring mit ihrem Töchterchen Edda

213. Frau Emmy Goering with her little daughter Edda.
This superb studio study of Goering's wife and child is unusual, in that it is not the work of Heinrich Hoffmann, the Party photographer. Produced for mass consumption, such images were used to promote the importance of family bonds and unity throughout the Reich. Emmy Goering moved to Munich after the war where she lived with her daughter until her death on 8 June, 1973.

214. Hermann Goering's country house near Berchtesgaden.
As previously stated Goering's home occupied one of the finest locations on the Obersalzberg, this postcard would appear to confirm that viewpoint. The footpath seen to the left of the house led towards the Berghof.

215. Interior of Goering's country house. Obersalzberg near Berchtesgaden.
The living room, while fashionably furnished, offered a level of comfort and intimacy not readily found inside Goering's other homes; 'Karinhalle' for example, the Field Marshal's fabulous country estate north of Berlin, was a huge, lavishly furnished palace when compared with his modest home on the Obersalzberg.

216. Interior of Goering's country house. Obersalzberg near Berchtesgaden.
Hermann Goering's study at his home on the Obersalzberg appears comfortable and unpretentious. Numerous pictures of his wife Emmy hang on the opposite wall while a portrait of Hitler sits on the desk.

217. Interior of Goering's country house. Obersalzberg near Berchtesgaden.
A view of the cosy seating area at the opposite end of the study. The small figure of a horse on the desk also appears in the previous postcard number 216. Accordingly, it forms a link between the two images, thus aiding the viewer in following the layout of the study more clearly.

218. Interior of Goering's country house. Obersalzberg near Berchtesgaden.
The traditionally furnished dining room appears functional and very homely. In contrast to his public persona, displaying a penchant for wearing flamboyant uniforms, these images of Goering's home offer a glimpse at an unfamiliar side to the Field Marshal's character. When beyond public view they would suggest a preference for understated simplicity, certainly at his Obersalzberg residence.

Other Buildings on the Obersalzberg

While Hitler's private residence on the Obersalzberg was, without doubt, the main attraction for all visitors to the mountain during the Third Reich (this included the many photographers whose work produced innumerable postcards), the fact remains that certain other buildings in the immediate area appear to have been neglected, at least photographically.

The home of Martin Bormann for example, the man who perhaps wielded the most authority on the Obersalzberg, compared with what we have already seen, might just as well have not existed. An explanation for the lack of postcards in this particular instance may be found in the character of Bormann himself. He disliked being photographed and it is true that few postcards exist depicting Bormann. Where these do exist, he is generally found lurking somewhere in the background. Furthermore, he appears to have been quite guarded in his private life, in which case he may not have permitted photographers access to his Obersalzberg home.

219. Dr Seitz children's convalescent home, Obersalzberg near Berchtesgaden.
The home of Dr Richard Seitz was located on the hillside opposite Hotel zum Türken. Occupying an elevated position the residence overlooked both the hotel and the Berghof. Martin Bormann, having purchased the property in 1936, then set about having it remodelled and enlarged as the family home. The interior was exquisitely furnished and provided all modern comforts. The house was badly damaged during the air raid in April, 1945; today no trace of the building remains.

220. The complete SS barracks, Obersalzberg.

The SS barracks were situated a short distance from the Berghof, lying beyond the crest of the hill behind the property. The complex comprised; living quarters, kitchens, administration offices, garages and training and sports halls. An underground rifle range was located beneath the large parade ground in the centre. There was even a post office nearby which, having survived the bombing in 1945, served until recently as a souvenir shop. The buildings seen here did not escape the air raid and were extensively damaged. Following demolition, the former parade ground was turned into a football field serving those who patronized the later restored Platterhof hotel.

The house observed in the background on the right and above the barracks is Landhaus (country house) Bormann following the renovations. Just below that, further right and almost completely obscured by trees, are the greenhouses. These provided fresh vegetables for those living on the mountain, including Hitler. A huge 138-room Intercontinental Hotel has recently been constructed on the hill above the spot where the greenhouses once stood.

Postcards depicting the SS complex are not commonly found due to the usual restrictions applicable regarding photography at military installations. To photograph the SS barracks on the Obersalzberg would have required permission from the highest level and, where granted, would have been subject to strict limitations for security reasons.

ersalzberg bei Berchtesgaden Georg Arnhold Klubheim. Bayer. Hochlan

221. Obersalzberg near Berchtesgaden Georg Arnhold Klubheim, Bavarian Highlands.

A better view of the property already observed in postcard number 190; before reconstruction, as is the case in this instance, and 193 following reconstruction in 1935. Thereafter it was known as Gästehaus Hoher Göll and was used as the Party guesthouse.

The building survived the 1945 bombing of the area relatively well; nonetheless looting played a large part in the demise of the interior through the post war years. The former guest house, having been largely demolished in the late 1990s was reborn to open as the new 'Dokumentation Obersalzberg' on 20 October, 1999. The centre provides a permanent exhibition of the history of the mountain region under the Nazis.

222. Theatre Hall Obersalzberg with Watzmann.

Few images depict the Theatre Hall on the Obersalzberg. Martin Bormann, on Hitler's instructions, ordered construction of the building which on completion could accommodate an audience of 2,000. Those forced labourers then working on the various projects in the region were permitted to attend performances in the Theatre Hall; entertainment consisted of the showing of newsreels and films in addition to the usual floor shows.

This rare postcard shows the building which, apart from the foundations and supporting columns was built entirely of wood. In this particular instance, and for some unknown reason, there is an individual standing on the roof of the building next to the chimney, thus we are better able to fully appreciate the scale of the structure. In the winter of 1943 the roof of the Theatre Hall suddenly collapsed under the immense weight of accumulated snow that had fallen in the region; less than one hour previously a large audience had attended an evening performance in the building.

The Destruction
of the Obersalzberg

The bombing of the Obersalzberg on 25 April, 1945, a mere twelve days prior to the actual surrender of all German forces on 7 May, now appears as nothing more than an act of wanton destruction. The objective of such an attack is far from clear. It certainly had little bearing on events elsewhere. The German surrender would have taken place regardless, and the effect on public morale at that point would have been negligible.

Nevertheless, it is obvious that the Nazi complex on the Obersalzberg would have been subject to a process of eradication at some point for political and ideological reasons. Consequently there remains little tangible evidence of Hitler's southern headquarters on the mountain today.

223. Hitler's Berghof Obersalzberg.
The bomb damaged remains of the Berghof following the air raid on the morning of 25 April, 1945. Every building situated on the Obersalzberg suffered during the attack; while some escaped with superficial damage, most were completely destroyed. The Berghof itself as we can see was badly damaged; looting also took its toll soon after the bombing. Hitler's former country residence remained in this state until 1952, when it was decided to demolish the ruin so as to leave no trace which might act as a focal point for future advocates of Nazi doctrine.

224. Berchtesgaden land, holiday country on the Obersalzberg.
Bearing an original caption that scarcely reflects the image this postcard gives a clear indication of the devastation inflicted on the area in April, 1945. In the centre we see what remains of Bormann's home, on the left is the damaged Platterhof hotel while on the lower right stands the Berghof. The overall impression is one of complete desolation extending far beyond the damaged structures to the very landscape itself.

225. Berchtesgaden, Obersalzberg. SS barracks and Platterhof.
In the foreground lie the completely destroyed and partly overgrown SS barracks. Behind that we see the badly damaged employees' accommodation block of the Platterhof hotel, later torn down. The lesser damaged main hotel building itself is furthest away. This was later restored only to be demolished in 2000 for reasons that still evade satisfactory explanation.

The Kehlsteinhaus (Eagle's Nest)

The Kehlsteinhaus is quite unique, a marvellous achievement for its architect, Roderich Fick, and the engineers and construction workers of the 1930s. The building should not be mistaken as is often the case, for Hitler's teahouse; it would have taken over two hours and all uphill to reach the Kehlsteinhaus on foot from the Berghof (a long way for a cup of tea). The Führer's private teahouse, which he visited almost daily when at the Berghof, as already stated, was located below the Berghof at Mooslahnerkopf, then about twenty minutes' walk distant; today it takes about forty-five minutes due to present restrictions lengthening the route. The Kehlsteinhaus has, on occasion, been referred to as the D-Haus, (House for Diplomats) as a number of VIPs were entertained there during the Third Reich period.

Perched as it is on a rocky outcrop on top of the Kehlstein Mountain at 1,834 metres (6,017 feet), the panoramic views on a clear day are truly magnificent. It was Martin Bormann who initiated the idea of the building; it would be something special to present to the Führer and in doing so he might gain further favour with Hitler. Discussions on the project began in April, 1937. However, such was the urgency expressed by (*Reichsleiter*) Reich Leader Bormann, that building work began before the end of the year.

The project had to be completed in time for Hitler's fiftieth birthday, on 20 April, 1939. Incredibly the work finished ahead of schedule at the end of 1938. Given the difficulties involved, the achievement almost defies belief. A new road had to be virtually blasted out of the mountain; this exceeded 6.5 kilometres (4 miles) when completed. All materials had to be moved to the site over the most difficult of terrains. During the winter progress was particularly slow and teams worked round the clock using searchlights during the hours of darkness.

To enter the building a tunnel almost 130 metres (over 400 feet) long was constructed through solid rock. At the end of this tunnel was a large waiting room where a lift, capable of carrying over forty people at a time, climbed another 130 metres to arrive inside the Kehlsteinhaus. The building consisted of reception/conference room, dining room, 'Scharitzstube' (Scharitz room, so called as it overlooks the Scharitzkehl), Hitler's study, guardroom, kitchen, a large basement and the usual facilities. Only the most experienced engineers and craftsmen had been employed on the project, together with the finest quality materials in its construction.

The estimated cost of this most extravagant of birthday presents was some 30 million Reichsmarks. When completed it is believed that around 3,500 workers had taken part in the task. Hitler's first visit to the Kehlsteinhaus was on 16 September, 1938; the NSDAP officially presented it to him on the occasion of his fiftieth birthday on 20 April, the following year. The Führer made fourteen official visits to the Kehlsteinhaus between 1938 and 1940 where visiting foreign heads of state were entertained and, most certainly, impressed by this triumph of German ingenuity.

On 18 October, 1938, the French Ambassador, André François-Poncet visited the Kehlsteinhaus. While later commenting on the experience he used the term 'Eagle's Nest' in his description of the event. In doing so he coined a new name for the building, a name that has been used ever since. Bormann, Goebbels, Himmler, Ribbentrop and Speer are but a few of the Party hierarchy to have visited the Eagle's Nest. On 3 June, 1944, Eva Braun organized for the wedding reception of her sister Gretl, to SS General Otto Hermann Fegelein to be held at the Kehlsteinhaus. Due to its location, being some distance from the Obersalzberg complex, the Kehlsteinhaus survived the air attack of April, 1945, unscathed. Having been returned to the Bavarian State in 1952 this historic building now serves as a mountain restaurant and remains a major tourist attraction in the area.

226. Berchtesgaden – The Kehlsteinhaus 1,840 metres above sea level.
This study of the magnificent Kehlsteinhaus probably dates from the early 1950s. Little changed, it remains today almost exactly as it appeared to Adolf Hitler on the occasion of his first visit on 16 September, 1938. Eva Braun frequently visited the Kehlsteinhaus, often accompanied by family members or friends such as Margerethe Speer or Gerda Bormann and her family.

227. Hitler's Eagle's Nest (1,832 metres).

This postcard again photographed in the 1950s shows the tunnel entrance which, in turn, leads to the large lift. What we see of the Kehlsteinhaus above is that part of the building, once the conference room, now a restaurant offering fabulous panoramic views of the entire region.

228. Hitler's Eagle's Nest (1,832 metres) Bavarian Alps.

The path leading from the Kehlsteinhaus towards the position adopted by the photographer carries on along the ridge of the mountain to arrive at the Mannlköpfe at 1,958 metres. This particular postcard offers a good overall view of the building, its location on the Kehlstein and, weather permitting, as is the case here, uninterrupted views of the surrounding mountains, in this instance towards the Lattengebirge.

The following images, numbers 229 to 240 are a unique contemporary collection of privately taken photographs showing the interior of the Kehlsteinhaus. To date I have not found any postcards depicting the interior of the building other than post war examples. Imagine my delight when unexpectedly stumbling upon this group of unusual photographs. Mercifully the standard payment of 'an arm and a leg' was not required in this instance. Obviously these images bear no original captions.

229. The dining room reveals the finest quality oak panelling and could accommodate as many as thirty guests around the long table.
The doorway at the opposite end of the room leads directly into the reception hall.

230. The reception hall in the Kehlsteinhaus was spacious and tastefully furnished; the large marble fireplace remains a most impressive feature in the room, now the dining/ function room.

231. Often incorrectly referred to as Eva Braun's room, the 'Scharitzkehlzimmer', finished in rare cembra pine panelling (as used in the Berghof dining room) still offers fabulous views towards both the Hoher Göll and the Königssee.

232. The Führer's Study located in the Kehlsteinhaus was actually never used by Hitler.

233. The guard room as used by the SS between 1938 and 1945. Inspection tours of the security fences in the area were regularly carried out from here. Today the former guard room performs a more peaceful role as a restaurant.

234. The then up to date and fully equipped kitchen stands ready for use.

235. These large brass door handles, in the form of two lions, were fixed to the large metal doors securing the entrance to the tunnel observed in postcard number 227. The original handles were taken by the Americans at the end of the war. Today's door handles are identical replacements.

236. A view of the 130 metre long, marble lined entrance tunnel looking back towards the doors, discussed in the previous caption number 235. The waiting room where one finds the lift by which one ascends to the Kehlsteinhaus is found close to where the photographer is standing in this particular instance.

237. The entrance to the large lift with highly polished solid brass interior and leather seating as observed from the aforementioned waiting room, which itself has a superb domed ceiling formed of large marble blocks.

238. A view of the 130 metre deep lift shaft, again constructed through solid rock.

239. This service tunnel, running parallel to the main entrance tunnel, accommodated all necessary electrical wiring and pipe-work for hot air systems, servicing both the entrance tunnel and lift shaft.

240. This large submarine engine was installed in a specially constructed underground engine room in 1938. Built in Bremerhaven its purpose was to supply backup power in the event of a breakdown in the normal power supply to the Kehlsteinhaus. The engine is fully operational and remains ready to perform its original function should the need arise.

Nazi Buildings Around Berchtesgaden

One might be forgiven for believing that construction in the region during the Nazi period was confined to the area of the Obersalzberg alone, but this is not so. Other buildings were constructed in and around the town of Berchtesgaden itself. When completed, these structures performed various functions including administration, accommodation, security and transport.

The railway station, as previously mentioned, had been rebuilt and enlarged to cope with the increased volume of visitors to the area. On re-opening in 1937, the new station was of a scale such as one might expect to find in a city at that time rather than a small alpine market town.

The postcards in the following section, numbers 241 to 254 cover the majority of these buildings, all of which remain standing today.

241. Reichs Chancellery with Watzmann and Hochkalter.

The Reichs Chancellery was constructed in 1936 under the supervision of Alois Degano, the architect responsible for both the Berghof and Goering's house on the Obersalzberg. Both Hitler and Bormann considered it a good idea to have a building of such status in the area performing dual diplomatic and governmental roles. The interior was in keeping with the status of the building, using the finest quality materials throughout. A large bunker beneath the Chancellery provided both shelter and supplies.

Generals Wilhelm Keitel and Alfred Jodl had houses close to the Chancellery; further buildings within the complex provided accommodation for staff and security personnel. The complex survived the war after which time it was used by the US for administration and accommodation of employees. The former Reichs Chancellery is situated in the suburb of Stangaß. It stands at the end of Urbanweg off Staatsstraße, approximately fifty minutes on foot from the centre of Berchtesgaden itself. The building has recently been converted into private flats. While the large eagle above the main doorway has been retained, the wreath held in its claws no longer displays the swastika.

242. With the eagle still in place above the doorway this is how the Reichs Chancellery appeared when photographed in 2004. The conversion work has been sympathetically carried out leaving the exterior of the building virtually unchanged.

243. Barracks Berchtesgaden-Strub with Hochkalter.

A view of the main gate of the Adolf Hitler Barracks as seen from the roadside. The scene remains virtually unchanged in the sixty odd years that have passed since this photograph was taken. With gaze fixed upon the Untersberg, the imposing stone lion continues to assert his authority over the approach to the complex. The barracks are located on Gebirgsjägerstrasse, off Ramsauer Straße about thirty-five minutes' walk (half of which is uphill) from Berchtesgaden, a short distance past the youth hostel.

244. Barracks Berchtesgaden-Strub with Untersberg.

This postcard shows soldiers standing in the grounds of the barracks just inside the main gate observed on the right. Constructed between 1936 and 1938 the barracks were home to *Gebirgsjägerregiment 100* (Mountain Infantry Regiment 100). The role of these troops was to provide both additional protection for the Nazi leaders and security for the area in general. The barracks also provided accommodation for high-ranking German officers during the latter part of the war. After 1945 the former Adolf Hitler Barracks were taken over by the US and put to various uses. Returned to German control in 1995 they are again home to a German regiment, the purpose for which they were originally constructed.

245. Berchtesgaden, Adolf Hitler Barracks.

Although similar to the previous postcard, number 244, this image appears strangely devoid of life. Having been photographed from a point further back inside the complex it depicts some of the grounds and accommodation blocks.

246. The same scene photographed in 2004; were it not for the large trees interrupting the view these two images are virtually identical. On approaching the main gate a notice warns that the taking of photographs is strictly forbidden, however, having sought permission and explained my reasons to the officer of the day, I was kindly permitted to carry out my request, a consideration for which I remain most grateful.

247. Barracks Berchtesgaden-Strub with Göll and Brett.
Here we look across the parade ground in the direction of the Hoher Göll. A large group of soldiers can be seen in the distance behind the flagpole. A small notice near the flagpole warns; 'Keep off the Grass'. Posted on 22.5.42, the reverse of this postcard carries greetings from a young soldier stationed at the barracks to his grandmother in Linz.

248. Reich's airport Bad Reichenhall-Berchtesgaden at Ainring.

Having opened in 1933, the small airport at nearby Ainring proved extremely useful to those requiring an audience with the Führer when he was residing on the Obersalzberg. Upon arrival at the airfield visitors completed the journey, approximately thirty-five kilometres (twenty-two miles) to the Berghof by car. Interestingly, Hitler personally explored the region to select Ainring as the location for the airport. Postcards of the airport at Ainring are rare. This example bears a postmark dated; 29.10.39. Less than ten days later, on 8 November, 1939, an unsuccessful attempt would be made on Hitler's life at the Bürgerbräu Keller in Munich. The Führer had travelled to Munich to take part in the annual celebrations and combined remembrance ceremony to honour the fallen comrades of the 1923 *Putsch*, to be held the following day, 9 November.

249. Adolf Hitler Youth Hostel Strub near Berchtesgaden.

This charming winter study depicts the youth hostel in Strub; it is located by the roadside not far from the army barracks mentioned in caption number 243. Having opening in 1936, the hostel helped to accommodate the vastly increased number of visitors to the region. Virtually unchanged the building continues to perform the role for which it was originally constructed. The hostel is located on Gebirgsjägerstrasse, approximately half an hour on foot from Berchtesgaden; to reach the barracks takes another five minutes along the same road. The latter half of the journey is a steep climb, however the scenery on arrival certainly compensates for the effort.

Führer und Baldur v. Schirach in der
f-Hitler-Jugendherberge in Berchtesgaden

250. The Führer and Baldur von Schirach in the Adolf Hitler Youth Hostel in Berchtesgaden.
Hitler, together with his entourage and Reich Youth Leader, Baldur von Schirach (on Hitler's left)
take their leave of the Youth Hostel near Berchtesgaden to the excited farewells of young people
gathered at the windows. The SS man behind Hitler dutifully carries the Führer's hat and coat.

251. Adolf Hitler Youth Hostel Berchtesgaden-Strub with Untersberg.
The entire region lies still and silent in the full grip of winter while the mighty Untersberg, bleak
and unwelcoming, dominates the background. On the reverse the sender explains how their room
is located on this side of the building, that cloud continues to obscure the view of the mountains,
the depth of snow in the area and finally, how beautiful the hostel is.

252. Adolf Hitler Youth Hostel, Berchtesgaden.
The towering Hoher Göll forms the backdrop for this summer view of that part of the hostel located close to the roadside. The Kehlsteinhaus, while obscured from view by the trees in this instance sits high on the mountain to the left of the Hoher Göll.

253. Part of the youth hostel as photographed in 2004. The perimeter wall next to the road together with the small fence on the right, as seen in the previous postcard number 252, no longer exist. Apart from these minor alterations little has changed since the building first opened its doors to travellers in 1936.

254. Walk on the Obersalzberg.
This caption for whatever reason is somewhat inaccurate, in that the property viewed here, then known as the Dietrich Eckart house (or Göllhäusl) is located approximately 2 kilometres (over 1 mile) from the Obersalzberg; being situated at end of Scharitzkehlstraße near Hinterbrand. In this instance we see Hitler (right) and Goering (left) in conversation with Minister of War and Commander in Chief of the Armed Forces, General Werner von Blomberg; a truly charming image that reveals the outstanding natural beauty of the area.

Section Four

Associates of the Obersalzberg:

Martin Bormann

❖

Eva Braun

❖

Joseph Goebbels

❖

Magda Goebbels

❖

Hermann Goering

❖

Rudolf Hess

❖

Heinrich Himmler

❖

Leni Riefenstahl

❖

Baldur von Schirach

❖

Albert Speer

❖

The Obersalzberg:
Tangible Remains Today

Associates of the Obersalzberg

he following postcard numbers 255 to 271, deal with some of those individuals with whom Hitler associated on the Obersalzberg. Whether professionally, or on a more personal level as members of the Führer's 'inner social circle', all spent considerable time in Hitler's company, both at the Berghof and in the surrounding area.

Martin Bormann

255. Opening the Party Congress.

This interesting postcard dating from the mid 1930s depicts the members of the Nazi 'Old Guard' attending the opening of the Annual Party Congress in Nuremberg.

From left to right they are: Dr Wilhelm Frick, Reich Minister of the Interior. Dr Paul Joseph Goebbels, Reich Minister of Public Enlightenment and Propaganda. Dr Hans Kerrl, Prussian Minister of Justice and Reich Minister without Portfolio. Franz Xavier Schwarz, Treasurer of the

NSDAP. Viktor Lutze, Chief of Staff of the SA. Adolf Hitler, Führer. Rudolf Hess, Deputy Führer. Julius Streicher, owner of *Der Stürmer* (The Storm), an illustrated anti-Semitic newspaper and Gauleiter (District leader) of Franconia. Behind Hess stands Lieutnant Wilhelm Brückner of the SA, adjutant to Hitler. Behind Streicher stands Julius Schaub, adjutant to Hitler. Finally, and on the extreme right, stands the man who has been described as 'the power behind the throne', *Reichsleiter* (Reich Leader) Martin Bormann.

Martin Bormann was born in Halberstadt, Lower Saxony, on 17 June, 1900. His father, a sergeant in a cavalry regiment and later civil servant, died when Martin was only four years old; his mother remarried some years later. Towards the end of the First World War, Martin Bormann was drafted and served as a gunner with Field Artillery Regiment 55, but saw little, if any action. With the war over Bormann found employment as an inspector in agriculture and joined the *Freikorps* (Free Corps). These groups of armed right-wing volunteers were opposed to, and would not accept, the harsh terms that the Versailles Treaty had imposed upon Germany. The *Freikorps* were secretly supported by the German Army, who itself advocated the 'stab in the back' theory for Germany's defeat.

During this period members of the Rossbach Freikorps unit in Mecklenburg, of which Bormann was a member, stood accused of the murder of one Walther Kadow who had allegedly betrayed Albert Leo Schlageter, a Freikorps officer (and later Nazi martyr) to the French forces of occupation in the Ruhr area. Schlageter had been tried on charges of espionage and sabotage and executed by the French on 26 May, 1923, near Düsseldorf. Martin Bormann for his part was found guilty of complicity in the affair and sentenced to one year in prison which he served in Leipzig. Shortly after his release in 1924, he made contact with and joined the NSDAP working in their press section in Thuringia. In 1928 he was promoted to work for the Chief of Staff of the SA. Bormann applied his considerable organizational skills to everything he did and soon acquired an excellent understanding of the workings of the Party.

In 1929 he married Gerda Bach, daughter of the President of the Party Court. Hitler acted as a witness at the ceremony, this act in itself confirmed Bormann's position within the Nazi hierarchy. Following Nazi success in the 1933 elections Martin Bormann was again promoted, this time to the position of deputy to Rudolf Hess. By 1937 Bormann had ingratiated himself into a position within Hitler's inner circle. His long suffering and devoted wife Gerda, herself popular with Hitler and an ardent Nazi, gave birth to no less than ten children, thus admirably fulfilling Party requirements to produce many offspring. Furthermore she tolerated and, to some extent condoned, her husband's many infidelities, which he openly admitted.

After 1933, Bormann's superior Rudolf Hess, was charged with the acquisition of land on the Obersalzberg to accommodate the Nazi programme of expansion in the area. Hess, not having time himself for this task handed the responsibility to his deputy. Bormann set about the job with his usual enthusiasm. To begin with he approached landowners correctly and with generous offers. If things became difficult he would adopt a more ruthless approach giving the landowner a stark choice; the offer, or the concentration camp. Until the flight of Hess to England in May, 1941, Bormann found himself appointed head of the newly created *Parteikanzlei* (Party Chancellery) which had replaced the former office of Rudolf Hess.

'Landhaus Bormann' his own home on the Obersalzberg overlooked the Berghof and Hotel zum Türken; it was extremely luxurious and boasted all modern conveniences. The traditional alpine exterior gave little indication of the sumptuous interior of the completely rebuilt former home of Dr Richard Seitz which Bormann had bought in 1936. Martin Bormann was indeed the power behind the throne on the Obersalzberg, but at a cost. He was disliked and mistrusted by the other Nazi leaders and hated by the local people. As his influence grew he cleverly placed his own people in positions of importance, to the extent that little information passed between the Führer and anyone else that Bormann did not know about. He alone was responsible for all building projects on the mountain estate and, following his appointment as Secretary to the Führer in 1943, Bormann enjoyed almost unlimited power, sending out 'Führer Orders' without fear of their origins being questioned. After this time Hitler was virtually the only person beyond Bormann's orders.

Martin Bormann lived only to serve his Führer; he seems to have had little else of real importance in his life save his devotion to, and total reliance on Hitler to maintain his status. Bormann, Hitler's shadow, omnipresent and ready to carry out the Führer's wishes with ruthless efficiency, withheld facts about the war situation from Hitler and denied high ranking military personnel access to the Führer. In his pursuit of power Bormann often deliberately misinterpreted Hitler's comments to suit his own ends. He outmanoeuvred all competitors in getting close to Hitler and remained loyal to the end.

On the occasion of the marriage of Adolf Hitler and Eva Braun on 29 April, 1945, Bormann acted as witness, thus returning the favour shown by the Führer who had performed this same function at Bormann's own wedding in 1929. Later that same day, Martin Bormann, the Führer's Secretary, was required to act as witness to Hitler's last will and political testament. In the matter of Hitler's will the faithful Bormann alone was appointed executor. Following the Führer's suicide on 30 April, 1945, Martin Bormann attempted to escape Berlin and for many years it was believed he had succeeded. However, in 1972 during construction work near the Lehrter station in Berlin, two skeletons were discovered; one of these was later identified as Dr Ludwig Stumpfegger, one of Hitler's personal physicians, the other was Martin Bormann. The escape had terminated barely half a mile from its starting point in the Reich's Chancellery bunker.

Eva Braun

Throughout the period of the Third Reich the subject of Eva Braun and her relationship with Adolf Hitler remained secret. With the exception of the Führer's 'inner circle', to the outside world she was simply another of Hitler's secretaries. The subject of politicians maintaining mistresses is nothing new, neither are their attempts to maintain secrecy or denial in such matters. Nonetheless the Führer's reputation had to be preserved; he had no wish to see his personal life investigated. When in the company of others, Hitler and Eva maintained certain formalities so as not to reveal their true relationship. In reality all members of Hitler's 'inner circle' knew the truth, but none of these ever broached the subject in their presence. Not until after 1945 would the secret of their long love affair be revealed to the world.

Consequently it is entirely reasonable to assume that postcards depicting Eva Braun were never produced. To have done so would have given her status; this would have led to questions, explanations and all manner of unnecessary complications which, in the end, might have tarnished the Führer's image. Few photographs exist showing Eva Braun and Adolf Hitler together, those that do exist are generally privately taken examples and these were certainly not for public scrutiny. On those rare occasions that Eva Braun does appear in official group photographs, she is presented and perceived as just another member of the Führer's staff.

Eva Braun, the daughter of a schoolteacher, came from a middle class background. She was born in Munich on 6 February, 1912. As a child Eva had little interest in schoolwork but was always very keen on sports. At about the age of fifteen, and by sheer coincidence, Eva attended a convent school at Simbach am Inn, (the river Inn forms a natural border between Germany and Austria). Simbach looks directly across the bridge connecting two countries towards Braunau am Inn, the birthplace of Adolf Hitler on the Austrian side.

Having spent a year at Simbach, Eva returned to Munich where she found employment for a short time as a doctor's receptionist. In late 1929 she answered an advert in a newspaper for a job as an assistant in a photographic studio. Heinrich Hoffmann, already Hitler's official photographer gave Eva the job. Within a few weeks of working at the studio Eva met Adolf Hitler for the first time;

256. Uncaptioned.

A privately taken photograph of Eva Braun at the Kehlsteinhaus with one of her two Scottish terriers, Stasi and Negus. Hitler often teased Eva referring to the dogs as 'carpet-sweepers', a term he initiated due to their short legs and long coats.

This is the only photograph I have of Eva Braun; is it not somewhat uncanny that in over ten years spent collecting the images seen on these pages, I should by pure chance, stumble upon it amongst a group of postcards in an antique shop in Berchtesgaden itself, while making a final effort to locate some last images prior to publication.

on that occasion he was introduced to her as 'Herr Wolf'. This was an alias used by Hitler during the early days; he had used the name years before around Berchtesgaden when banned from public speaking, perhaps to keep his whereabouts secret.

There was an immediate attraction on both sides. Eva and Adolf began to meet and many letters were exchanged between them. Later, in 1932, as the demands of politics took up more and more of his time, Eva saw much less of Hitler. In November that year during a spell of depression, Eva attempted suicide using her father's pistol. The attempt failed but immediately brought Hitler to her bedside in a Munich clinic. Eva later tried to dismiss the event as nothing more than an accident while examining the gun.

With Hitler being elected German Chancellor in 1933, Eva became a more frequent visitor to the Obersalzberg, under the guise of just another of the Führer's secretaries. Her parents, who it must be said Hitler always treated with the utmost respect, reluctantly accepted the relationship between their daughter and the Führer. Hitler's half-sister, Angela, had been installed as housekeeper at Haus Wachenfeld in the mid 1920s. However, she and Eva did not see eye to eye and Angela finally left in 1936. Eva, a girl who demanded nothing of Hitler other than his attention and affection and who became melancholic during his absences, thereafter assumed the role of housekeeper on the Obersalzberg.

Eva's only vice was something that Hitler detested; smoking. Somehow she managed to keep this a secret from him or he pretended never to know. Always a keen sportswoman, Eva enjoyed gymnastics, swimming, climbing and skiing which she did on the Obersalzberg and surrounding areas. The Königssee was a favourite venue for activities like swimming and picnics. She maintained a keen interest in photography, something she had picked up while working for Hoffmann. Shopping was something she delighted in, particularly clothes; as a result she was probably the most fashionably dressed woman in the area. Eva's closest friends on the Obersalzberg were Margerethe Speer and Gerda Bormann; all three spent much time in each others company. Eva's family and friends were frequent visitors at the Berghof and, during Hitler's absence, they often held parties where Eva had an opportunity to indulge her love of dancing.

While totally uninterested in politics Eva had total trust in Hitler's abilities. The Führer, it must be said, showed great affection for Eva during his many long absences through the war by way of daily telephone calls and much letter writing. Those who knew Eva through these years said she lost neither her naturalness nor her warm personality. Loyal to the last and, against the Führer's wishes Eva left the relative safety of the Berghof and travelled to Berlin to be with him at the end, arriving there on 15 April. There in the Führer bunker beneath the crumbling city, the man to whom she had devoted her life finally married her in recognition of that devotion and loyalty, on 29 April, 1945. Eva Hitler maintained her composure to the last. The following day, Monday, 30 April, at about 3.30 in the afternoon, having retired to their private suite, she and her husband committed suicide together, Eva by taking cyanide, while Hitler shot himself. On Hitler's prior instructions their bodies were then burned side by side in the Reich's Chancellery garden.

Joseph Goebbels

257. Reich Minister Dr Goebbels.
This fine Hoffmann study of Goebbels (opposite) portrays an extremely confident man who, while he appears relaxed before the camera, displays the calm authority of one who is obviously well aware of the extent of his far-reaching power.

258. The family of Reich Minister Dr. Goebbels.
Probably taken in early 1938, this particularly captivating photograph shows Joseph and Magda Goebbels together with four of their six children; behind Goebbels stands Magda's son from her first marriage, Harald. While beautifully posed and photographed this image communicates the impression of a happy and united family.

RER u. Dr. Goebbels mit Töchterchen Helga

259. The Führer and Dr Goebbels with his little daughter Helga.
This photograph was taken by the entrance to the Goebbels' family home at Schwanenwerder.
Helga, whom Goebbels is holding, was a particular favourite of the children with Hitler.

Paul Joseph Goebbels was born on 29 October, 1897, in the small town of Rheydt in the Rhineland. As a child he had suffered polio leaving him with a crippled left foot and weakened leg. Goebbels was a clever boy who compensated for his physical disability by immersing himself in books. As a young man he had studied in Munich. Later, while on a return visit to the city in 1922 he heard Adolf Hitler speak for the first time. Goebbels immediately joined the Party, such was the effect of this first encounter with Hitler. This event transformed Goebbels into the dedicated follower he would remain for virtually the rest of his life.

In 1926 the Berlin faction of the Party was losing ground to the Communists. Hitler immediately dispatched Goebbels to the city appointing him *Gauleiter* (District Leader) of Berlin. Hitler rightly believed that Goebbels' energies could be put to best use in the capital where the NSDAP was in a state of disarray and failing to attract new members. In the twelve months that followed Goebbels increased Party numbers dramatically through some excellent campaigning, numerous street battles and a gift for inflammatory speechmaking. Through this period of upheaval Goebbels identified propaganda as the 'key' to political success. His reward for winning Berlin back for the Party was to be appointed head of propaganda; a role tailor-made for Goebbels and vice versa.

The newly appointed Goebbels set about his work with unbridled enthusiasm. He transformed meetings and rallies into dramatic events by introducing music, flags, marching and lighting effects. Future events became innovative visual masterpieces, overseen by Goebbels, the propaganda craftsman. Continually striving to increase Party numbers and awareness, Goebbels was now in a position to win hearts and minds through more subtle means. With the Nazis emerging victorious from the 1933 elections, Hitler appointed his faithful servant 'Minister for Public Enlightenment and Propaganda', with offices located opposite the Reichs Chancellery in Berlin.

Goebbels next move was to gain control over the press and radio; once achieved these were put to work for the Party. Then it was cinema, theatre and publishing. Goebbel's power over what was seen, heard and thought was immense. Nor was the relatively new phenomenon of television overlooked. The Nazis were quick to recognize the potential of television, initiating the world's first public service broadcasts, then, having cleverly installed television sets in community centres, the Party proceeded to intoxicate the masses. Hitler's Propaganda Minister understood very well that the people could be seduced by using all the means at his disposal; he also knew just how to achieve that end. He once said, 'this is the secret of propaganda; the saturation of a group of people, with propagandist ideas, without them even knowing it. Of course propaganda has a goal, but the goal must be so clever and so brilliantly concealed, that the people who are to be influenced by it don't notice anything.' Goebbels' unshakeable belief in this statement allowed him to make it reality.

Despite everything written and proclaimed by Goebbels he was not in favour of war. He realized the risks involved, however, he fully accommodated the new requirements necessitated by war when it came. As things progressed he became even more convinced of the importance of his own role, and, as the tide of war turned against Germany he was one of the few Nazi leaders who personally visited scenes of devastation. He worked tirelessly to inspire the people to further efforts and greater sacrifices through his many speeches, broadcasts and writing.

Following the attempt on the Führer's life at Rastenburg, East Prussia on 20 July, 1944, it was Joseph Goebbels who, with skilful oratory managed to persuade those sent to arrest him that Hitler was still alive; this single act quelled the revolt in Berlin. Secretly, Goebbels had few doubts about the war and its inevitable outcome. On 22 April, 1945, Goebbels, his wife Magda and their six children took refuge in the Führer's bunker beneath the Reichs Chancellery. The situation quickly deteriorated. Adolf Hitler and his wife Eva committed suicide on 30 April. The following day, 1 May, 1945, at about 8.30 in the evening, Joseph Goebbels concluded that life without his Führer was not worth living; accordingly, and to avoid the family being taken prisoners, Joseph and Magda, with the aid of two of Hitler's personal physicians still in the bunker, poisoned their six children.

This gruesome task accomplished they exited the bunker and, standing in what remained of the Chancellery garden, ordered an SS man to shoot them both in the back of the head, which he did. Their bodies were then set alight with what remaining fuel could be found close to where the remains of the Führer and his wife lay. In conclusion, it must be said, regardless of what one might think of Joseph Goebbels, he was the originator of modern, intensive propaganda techniques. He used his remarkable skills in that area to incredible effect and, so successfully, that numerous post war politicians have imitated many of those techniques, if in a somewhat diluted form.

Magda Goebbels

260. The family of Dr Goebbels.

This delightful studio image shows Magda Goebbels surrounded by her children; all the children from her marriage to Joseph Goebbels had been given names beginning with the letter 'H' in honour of Hitler.

Front row left to right; Helmut (02.10.35), Hedda (05.05.38), Heidi, on mother's knee (29.10.40), Holde (19.02.37) and Helga (01.09.32). Back row; Hilde (12.04.34) and Harald, the son from her first marriage, born in 1921. The Goebbels children adored Harald, a lieutenant in the *Luftwaffe* who ended the war as a prisoner of the British, having been captured in Italy.

261. Uncaptioned.
Yet another image from the same photographic session. This time Hitler's devoted Propaganda Minister, Joseph Goebbels joins Magda and their children in an image where some of the children are finding it rather difficult to contain their restlessness; typical of all children on such occasions.

Magda Goebbels was born in Berlin, on 11 November, 1901. Her mother, Auguste Behrend, although some controversy surrounds the issue, was unmarried. Her father, Oskar Ritschel was an engineer. The child, christened Johanna Maria Magdalena, was raised and educated from the age of five in a convent at Thild in Belgium; in 1908 she moved to the convent at Vilvoorde just north of Brussels. When the First World War began in 1914, Magda returned to Germany. At the age of eighteen she met and married Günther Quandt, a wealthy businessman twenty years her senior. The marriage produced one child, Harald, however the relationship was not a happy one and the couple divorced amicably in 1929.

In 1930 Magda Quandt attended a Nazi election campaign meeting at the Sportpalast in Berlin; Joseph Goebbels was one of those speaking at the event. Completely overwhelmed by his oratory Magda left the meeting converted to the cause. They were to meet a short time later at one of the Party's offices where Magda had then found employment. Goebbels immediately showed an interest in the attractive young blonde. As time passed he realized that Magda would be a very good catch; her background and contacts would bring an air of respectability to the Party. Magda offered access to areas of the upper classes where the Nazis still struggled to make a favourable impression.

Magda Quandt and Joseph Goebbels were married in December, 1931, with Hitler in attendance as witness. The Führer was actually very fond of Magda; she was intelligent, confident, charming and showed an interest in the Party. Hitler realized these valuable attributes could be of great use. Magda represented the perfect Nazi image of German womanhood; as such she supported Hitler acting as hostess at parties and official functions. In time her role became that of unofficial first lady. The six children from her marriage to Goebbels were filmed and photographed in and around their home at Schwanenwerder; these images were then used as representative of the model Nazi family, with Magda the ideal mother and homemaker.

In 1938 the continuing womanizing of her husband finally brought Magda to breaking point. Goebbels had declared his love for Lida Barova, a Czech actress; his latest conquest. On hearing that he planned to leave her and the children Magda threatened divorce and went straight to Hitler. The Führer would not hear of his Propaganda Minister getting divorced, thus shattering the perfect image of Nazi family life. Hitler fully realized the value of Goebbels' devotion to him and the abilities he possessed. Goebbels finally bowed to the Führer's wishes and the scandal was averted.

Madga Goebbels also remained totally loyal to Hitler; in the end neither she nor her husband could see any point in a life without their Führer, or the Party. Magda feared for her children; if captured they might be the victims of a terrible revenge and, given that it was the Russians who were then surrounding Berlin, this fear may not have been unjustified. On 1 May, 1945, with Hitler already dead, Magda attended the children in the Führer bunker with SS Dental Surgeon, Dr Kunz. While explaining to the children that they were being given an injection for health reasons, Dr Kunz administered injections of morphine to each of them. A short time later while they were asleep, she returned with SS Surgeon, Dr Ludwig Stumpfegger, one of Hitler's personal physicians and together they placed poison into the mouths of the children. A truly desperate decision taken in desperate circumstances, one cannot begin to imagine the anguish and sense of total loss of a mother driven to such an act. Magda and Joseph Goebbels then exited the bunker, their own lives ended by the entrance to the bunker in the Reich's Chancellery garden.

Hermann Goering

262. The Reich Marshal.
Goering behind his desk at *Luftwaffe* headquarters in the Wilhelmstrasse in Berlin. The building stands today virtually unchanged.

HERMANN GÖRING

263. Hermann Goering, General Field Marshal.
Goering's demeanour is that of a man set on his course, determined, unyielding, immovable.

Most of the medals and awards he proudly wears were earned during the First World War while in command of *Jagdstaffel 27* (Fighter Squadron 27), and later the famous Richthofen 'Flying Circus' following the death of the 'Red Baron'.

264. Reich Minister Goering.

Postcards depicting Goering in civilian clothes are rare; he was a man who much preferred being photographed while wearing uniform. In this instance, Goering more resembles a film star of the period rather than a minister in Hitler's government; nevertheless this is certainly a striking image.

REICHSMINISTER GÖRING

Hermann Wilhelm Goering was born on 12 January, 1893, in Rosenheim, east of Munich. His father, a diplomat, had served in the German colonies. Hermann Goering entered military academy at the age of twelve. On leaving four years later he attended officer training college at Lichtenfelde near Berlin, where he remained until passing out aged nineteen. With the Goering family now settled in Munich, Hermann joined the 112th Prince Wilhelm Regiment. However, following certain 'irregularities' and, near the mark 'escapades' his most ardent wish to transfer to the air force was finally granted. This was largely due to the intervention of influential friends working on his behalf behind the scenes.

During the First World War, Goering proved himself a brave and able pilot earning command of *Jagdstaffel 27* (Fighter Squadron 27). He went on to win Germany's highest honour the *Pour la Mérite*. In July, 1918, following the death of the 'Red Baron', Hermann Goering assumed command of the famous 'Richthofen' squadron, which he led until the end of hostilities. Following the German surrender Goering travelled extensively in Denmark and Sweden demonstrating Fokker aircraft, it was during this time that he met his first wife, Carin von Kantzow.

On returning to Munich in 1922, Goering encountered Adolf Hitler and, having joined the Party, he played an important role in the reorganization of the SA. Goering possessed many qualities that made him a valuable asset to the Party, and its leader. On taking part in the Munich *Putsch* on 9 November, 1923, Goering was badly wounded. He fled to Austria where he received medical treatment, however this led to a morphine addiction, a condition from which he would never fully recover. In addition, the treatment had also affected his glands, so that on his return to Germany Goering had put on considerable weight. In 1928 he was re-admitted to the Party hierarchy and elected to the Reichstag. His wife Carin, died of tuberculosis on 17 October, 1931, leaving him completely devastated.

Gradually coming to terms with the loss of his wife, Goering launched himself into fund-raising and the recruitment of new Party members, both of which he did extremely well, attracting wealthy and influential friends from industry and the nobility. When Hitler became Chancellor in 1933, it was one of the happiest moments in Goering's life. Having played a major role in their success behind the scenes, the loyal and devoted Goering was aptly rewarded and given a number of important ministerial posts, including that of Reich Commissioner for Air. This allowed Goering to pursue his intention to create a strong air force for Germany, the *Luftwaffe.*

On 10 April, 1935, Hermann Goering married the well known actress, Emmy Sonnemann. With Hitler acting as best man, the whole event featured as a high point in the Nazi calendar at the time. The 'Four Year Plan', introduced in 1933 to tackle the nations unemployment and economic problems, was overseen by Goering, as was a second 'Four Year Plan' introduced in 1936, this time aimed at reducing Germany's dependence on imported raw materials together with an increase in military development. Hermann Goering correctly believed that Germany could not win a long drawn out war. However he fully committed the *Luftwaffe* to the conflict in 1939 with initial marked success. He attempted to impress upon Hitler the importance of defeating Britain, but the Führer held the belief that peace with Britain could be negotiated; had Churchill not become British Prime Minister in May, 1940, this might have remained a possibility.

With the defeat of Germany's old enemy France, in June, 1940, Goering was promoted to the rank of Field Marshal. Ironically, had Hitler listened to Goering's ideas on how to conduct the air war against Britain, it is almost certain that German air supremacy would have been achieved. Again, Goering was against war with Russia, he concluded that the Luftwaffe was not equipped for a war on two fronts and that Germany must first deal with England. As the war progressed and things began to go badly for Germany, Goering detached himself more and more from the conflict, thereafter immersing himself in collecting all kinds of treasures from the occupied countries. In early 1945, and as a result of the deteriorating military situation, Goering was forced to transport this huge collection to Berchtesgaden by train, where it went into storage.

With the ever increasing destruction of German cities through Allied bombing, Hitler finally lost all faith in Goering whom he blamed personally for the inability of the *Luftwaffe* to protect the Reich. In the final days, as the Russians tightened their grip on Berlin, Goering was persuaded as 'Hitler's successor' to act, by General Koller. Sending a telegram to Hitler in Berlin, Goering offered his services to negotiate with the Western Allies in an attempt to arrive at some sort of peace. Hitler's initial response to the idea was controlled. However, following deliberate misrepresentation of the idea and much back-stabbing by Goering's arch enemy Martin Bormann, Hitler flew into a rage ordering that Goering be stripped of all authority and arrested for treason.

The faithful Goering, always popular with the German people, was captured by the Americans on 9 May, 1945. When trials began in Nuremberg in November, 1945, Hermann Goering was the one man who stood out and dominated the trials from amongst the surviving Nazi leaders. He was found guilty on all counts and sentenced to death by hanging; his request to be shot by firing-squad was denied. Goering however, managed to cheat the hangman; he was found dying in his cell on 15 October, 1946, having taken poison he had managed to conceal, just hours before the sentence was to be carried out.

Rudolf Hess

265. Deputy Führer Reich Minister Rudolf Hess.
This photograph portrays Hess as he has been generally perceived, serious and uncompromising.

266. Reich Minister Rudolf Hess Deputy Führer with his son Wolf-Rüdiger.
This truly fabulous image sees Hess, the family man, playing with his small son, Wolf-Rüdiger (born on 18 November, 1937) at the family home at Harlaching on the outskirts of Munich. Displaying all the affection of a father for his son, one can only speculate as to the number of times Hess would have reflected on such moments as he languished in Spandau Prison until his death in 1987.

267. Reich Minister Rudolf Hess, Deputy Führer, with his son Wolf-Rüdiger.
Joyful and carefree, Hess expects his son may fall from the shutter at any moment and, like any loving father, he is prepared to catch the boy instantly should this happen. These photographs were taken just a short time before Hess's fateful flight to Britain on 10 May, 1941.

Walter Richard Rudolf Hess, was born in Alexandria, on 26 April, 1894. His father, a wealthy businessman living in Egypt, was a strict disciplinarian as far as his children were concerned. Hess was educated at a German school in Alexandria until 1908, when his father bought property in Bavaria where the family would spend part of the year. It was around this time that Rudolf Hess's education began in Germany. Coming from an upper middle class background Hess, as a young man, had been well educated and got on well with people.

During the First World War, Rudolf Hess was wounded three times while serving as a lieutenant in a Bavarian infantry regiment. Following his release from hospital on the last occasion he joined the Imperial Flying Corps; however the war ended just as he was completing his training and he left the service. In 1920 Hess entered university in Munich while at the same time reviving an earlier interest in politics; on hearing Hitler speak at a meeting of the NSDAP he joined the movement. Hess soon became one of Hitler's closest and most trusted comrades; the two men spent much time in each others' company discussing various topics at length. On the morning of the Munich *Putsch*, on 9 November, 1923, Hess marched beside Hitler and, while many of the Nazi leaders were arrested Hess managed to escape to Austria. However, following Hitler's trial and sentencing he returned to Germany and was, in turn, sentenced to eighteen months for his part in the event.

It was while serving their sentences together in Landsberg Prison that Hitler dictated *Mein Kampf* (My Struggle) to Hess, who acted as secretary and assistant to Hitler. Their incarceration resulted in a close bond between the two men. Hess, having played a major part in the electoral campaign that swept the Nazis to victory in January, 1933, was rewarded for his loyalty later that year when he was appointed Deputy Führer on 21 April. Rudolf Hess has been described as cool, polite and reserved, yet he was a man of simple taste who enjoyed books and music; he did not indulge in luxuries. The Deputy Führer was a regular visitor at the Berghof where, when not relaxing, he spent considerable time discussing policies with Hitler.

Whether or not Hitler knew of Hess's planned flight to Scotland on 10 May, 1941, is even today a matter for speculation. However the two men spent four hours in private discussion just days prior to the Deputy Führer's departure. Suffice to say that there were highly placed individuals in Britain, both inside and outside government, who still wished to arrive at peace with Germany at that time. Whatever the truth, Hitler was furious when he learned of the disappearance of his Deputy. It is generally accepted that Hitler later came to realize that Hess's flight was a truly selfless gesture; an attempt at least to secure peace with England. That attempt, if successful, would have afforded Germany the best opportunity to defeat Soviet Russia by no longer having to fight a war on two fronts. Hitler later confided to those closest to him that he greatly missed Hess, who, he went on to say was one of only a few individuals to whom he had a strong personal attachment.

Much controversy surrounds the departure of Hess from Augsburg in 1941, and several theories have been proposed in this area. One such theory suggests that Britain was not his destination, but a neutral country where he intended to open negotiations which might lead to peace. Another to be put forward and, backed by unsettling evidence, suggests that the Messerschmitt Me 110 in which Hess left Germany was not the same aircraft to arrive in Scotland. Others suggest that the man who stood trial at Nuremberg in 1946 was in fact not Hess, but a double and that this individual played out his role to the end for fear of reprisals against his own family should he fail to do so. It is certainly true that the man claiming to be Rudolf Hess, who remained a prisoner of the British until the end of the war, bore a strong physical resemblance to Hess. On the other hand it has been stated that discrepancies, in both known medically recorded facts and traits in personality and ability, were blatantly apparent.

The secrecy and deliberately misleading comments of successive British governments then and since, have only served to fuel increasing doubts and unanswered questions. These questions do not abate; the mysterious death of prisoner number 7 at Spandau Prison in Berlin on 17 August, 1987, leaves the file wide open. Why were a number of appeals for the release of the prisoner between 1947 and 1966 all refused? Why, was Hess alone kept in Spandau until he died when all other Nazi prisoners, given life sentences, had been released? Probably because of what he knew; knowledge is a dangerous thing when feared by those it might embarrass, dishonour or destroy if ever made public.

268. The Reichsführer SS visiting SS Panzer Grenadier Regiment (Armoured Infantry Regiment) *'Der Führer'* with Brigadeführer Dr Otto Wächter and Brigadeführer Friedrich Freitag.

Der Führer was a combat unit of the 2nd SS Panzer Division *Das Reich*. This Division produced more Knight's Cross winners than any other, sixty-nine in total.

A typical SS Division consisted of some 15,000 fighting men together with between 5,000 and 6,000 support personnel. The reverse of this postcard bears a large contemporary regimental stamp which has subsequently been completed by hand, recording the details of the event.

Heinrich Himmler

Heinrich Himmler was born in Munich on 7 October, 1900. His father, the highly respected deputy principal of a reputable grammar school in Landshut, north-east of Munich, had taught Prince Heinrich of Bavaria, after whom the young Himmler was named; Prince Heinrich having graciously consented to be the boy's godfather. Heinrich Himmler was brought up in a well-to-do and devout Roman Catholic home, in an atmosphere of tolerance and respect. He had been well educated and had not been personally affected by the horrors of the First World War other than having observed the return of maimed and wounded soldiers from the various fronts. Nonetheless, his most ardent wish was to be a soldier and, when only seventeen and still under age, he joined the 11th Bavarian Infantry Regiment as an officer-cadet. Hostilities ended prior to Himmler completing his training, whereupon he returned to his studies in Munich to obtain a diploma in agriculture.

It was to remain a source of regret throughout Himmler's life that he had not seen active service during the First World War. Descriptions of Himmler as a young man range from polite, respectful and considerate; to harmless and rather shy. Even in later life he maintained this reluctance to appear in the limelight, preferring to remain in the background and avoid publicity. Ernst Röhm, one of Hitler's earliest and closest comrades, regularly visited those places frequented by students in Munich in the hope of finding suitable new members; Heinrich Himmler was but one of many recruited to the NSDAP by Röhm in this way in 1920. Röhm would become Himmler's mentor through these early years. However, following the 'Röhm Purge' in late June, 1934, Hitler would become the figure idolized by Himmler.

[Röhm, had become a threat to Hitler's authority. He had enjoyed the support of the general population and remained capable of mobilizing more SA members than any other of the Nazi leadership. Unwilling to submit totally to Hitler's authority, Ernst Röhm and certain of his supporters were eliminated to avoid a second revolution through the ever-increasing strength of the SA who were loyal to Röhm. The Party justified Röhm's removal by stating that the former SA chief had been discovered plotting a coup.]

A total believer in Nazi doctrine, Himmler marched beside Hitler during the unsuccessful *Putsch* on 9 November, 1923 somehow managing to avoid both injury and arrest. In 1928 Himmler married Margarethe Boden. The marriage produced one child, a daughter, Gudrun. However the relationship proved difficult and the couple separated shortly after the birth of their child. Bringing a particularly methodical approach to all tasks and applying great attention to detail, Himmler worked with a patient tenacity to please his superiors. In 1929 Hitler appointed Himmler, Reichsführer SS, following the resignation of his predecessor, Erhard Heiden. The new Reichsführer threw himself into this new role with dedication and determination and, almost immediately, introduced strict new recruitment criteria for the SS (*Schutzstaffel*). Hitler showed little interest at the time, but gave his approval to the expansion of the élite corps who would later prove fanatically loyal in both their actions on the battlefield and in their role as personal bodyguard to the Führer.

The *Waffen SS* (Military SS) were to prove exceptional soldiers; so much so, that where the regular army got bogged down or, where there existed a stalemate on any front, it was the SS who were called upon to smash through, which they generally did with their usual enthusiasm. Himmler eventually enlarged the SS from three, to thirty-eight divisions. While the majority of these were fighting units, there were certainly some units involved in work at the various concentration camps where even the Reichsführer was personally involved in formulating methods of eliminating various 'undesirables'. On Hitler's orders, Himmler had established the first concentration camp at Dachau, north of Munich, in 1933; the Reichsführer was later given control and expansion of all concentration camps and their various functions. Heinrich Himmler acquired control of the *Sicherheitsdienst 'SD'* (SS Security Service) and the *Geheime Staatspolizei 'Gestapo'* (Secret State Police) in 1934 and, finally, control of all German Police in 1936. The subjects of astrology and Aryan legend held a fascination for the Reichsführer and he had maintained an interest in breeding and genetics from his student days.

By 1944 Himmler realized that Germany could no longer hope to win the war. By the spring of 1945 and, with the end in sight, Himmler began to think in terms of 'personal survival' and to that end began making tentative approaches towards the Western Allies in the hope of brokering a deal. One attempt towards the end of April, 1945, involved Count Folke Bernadotte, a Swedish nobleman working with the Red Cross; he would act as intermediary and met Himmler at the Swedish Consulate in Lübeck. The Reichsführer offered to surrender all German forces in the west to General Eisenhower, while opening the concentration camps to the Red Cross; the offer was refused. Incidentally, Count Bernadotte was killed by Jewish extremists in Jerusalem, in September, 1948, while attempting to negotiate peace between Jews and Arabs in the region.

With Hitler still unaware of Himmler's approaches to the Allies, the Reichsführer attended the celebrations for the Führer's fifty-sixth birthday in the Reich's Chancellery bunker in Berlin on 20 April, 1945. On later learning of Himmler's betrayal, Hitler was absolutely furious. He stripped the Reichsführer of all authority and ordered his arrest on sight. With the war in Europe at an end Himmler, disguised in tattered sergeant's uniform, wearing an eye-patch and having shaved off his moustache was arrested along with his companions by British soldiers while attempting to mingle with other prisoners near Bremervörde, west of Hamburg on 21 May, 1945. Two days later, on 23 May, 1945, having revealed his true identity and while being medically examined and searched for possible means of suicide at a camp near Lüneburg, Heinrich Himmler bit down hard on the vial of cyanide hidden in his mouth and died immediately. The former Reichsführer SS was subsequently buried on 26 May, in an unmarked grave in one of the many forested areas surrounding Lüneburg.

Leni Riefenstahl

Leni Riefenstahl was born in Berlin, on 22 August, 1902 and, following a successful career as a dancer with the Russian ballet, she became drawn to the world of film acting. Founding her own film company in 1931, she received recognition for her work almost immediately. *Das blaue Licht* (The Blue Light) which she wrote, produced and directed with Riefenstahl herself playing the lead role, won a gold medal at the Venice Biennale in 1932, establishing her name and paving the way to future success.

In February, 1932, Fräulein Riefenstahl, on attending her first ever political meeting heard Hitler speak in the Berlin Sportpalast. Shortly after the event she wrote to Hitler requesting a meeting, which took place soon after. Hitler much admired the charming, beautiful perfectionist and suggested that when the Nazis achieved power she must make his films. Riefenstahl replied that she could not make politically motivated films; furthermore, she would not join the Party. Hitler would not be put off. While continuing to declare his enormous respect for her as an artist and, applying his not to be underestimated power of persuasion, Leni Riefenstahl finally succumbed, and was appointed director/producer for Party film-making.

Riefenstahl's best known work during the Third Reich period is undoubtedly *Triumph des Willens* (Triumph of the Will) covering the 1934 Party Rally at Nuremberg. This film is testament to the quality of her work and expertise. It remains the single, greatest, directly politically motivated film of all time, a three hour long spectacular which, even today, stands apart as an incredible feat for the period. Riefenstahl overcame many difficulties to produce a masterpiece which captured the event superbly.

Needless to say, Hitler was delighted with the result. Riefenstahl's newfound status meant she was invited to many Party functions and went on outings with Hitler and his inner circle, including visits to the Obersalzberg and the Berghof. It has been suggested that Reifenstahl and Hitler had a personal relationship. This she always denied and no proof that any such relationship took place has ever been produced. Joseph Goebbels, strangely and for some unexplained reason, perhaps jealousy, always seemed to resent Riefenstahl's direct access to Hitler and her friendly relationship with him.

Riefenstahl continued to work in film after the war, but never again quite so successfully. She could never shake off the memories of her connection to the Third Reich. However she insisted on her having had no knowledge of any wrongdoing during the period of her film work under Hitler. Leni Riefenstahl died quietly at her home in Pöcking near the Starnberger See, some thirty-two kilometres (20 miles) south-west of Munich, on 9 September, 2003, having achieved the amazing age of 101.

269. Leni Riefenstahl.
A delightful studio study of the glamorous Leni Riefenstahl dating from the 1920s.

Baldur von Schirach

Baldur von Schirach was born in Berlin, on 9 March, 1907. In 1924 he moved to Munich to continue his studies and it was there, in the birthplace of the NSDAP, that he fell in with a group of Nazis. Von Schirach came from an upperclass background, was well educated and made a favourable impression with the Nazis; as a result he was appointed head of the National Socialist German Students League in 1929. The young man's abilities and enthusiasm did not go unnoticed and, in 1931, Hitler gave him the post of Youth Leader of the National Socialist Party. Hitler became German Chancellor in 1933. Shortly after von Schirach was appointed head of the *Hitler Jugend* (Hitler Youth).

The Hitler Youth was the male branch of the German Youth movement. Hitler believed that the survival of his planned 'Thousand-Year Reich' depended on the indoctrination and enthusiasm of the young. The family backgrounds of all applicants were carefully vetted, thus ensuring 'racial purity', an important part of the process. New members, boys aged between fourteen and eighteen were admitted to the organization on the same day each year at a ceremony attended by a high ranking Party official; that day was 20 April, the date of Hitler's birthday. The education of Hitler Youth was strictly controlled and monitored. On leaving, individuals moved through other organizations under Party control. Eventually, having been fully indoctrinated with Nazi ideals, they joined the armed forces. This meant in effect that the Party could exert a strong influence over an individual during his formative years.

Over 50,000 members of the Hitler Youth paraded before their Führer at the Annual Nuremberg Rally in September, 1935. While addressing this gathering, Hitler emphasized the importance of their role in his new Germany and how one day they would inherit everything the Party was then creating. After 1936 the Hitler Youth became a state agency. This meant that every German youth who had been successfully vetted, was expected to join. Baldur von Schirach had overall control of the Hitler Youth; an important position. As such his power and influence during that time should not be underestimated.

When war came von Schirach volunteered and saw action on the western front, however, following a reduction of conflict on that front, he returned to Germany in 1940. Hitler, concerned that von Schirach might become too powerful if returned to his former position, appointed him *Gauleiter* (District Leader) of Vienna. Baldur von Schirach was a frequent visitor to the Berghof. On one occasion his wife Henriette, a daughter of Hitler's photographer Hoffmann, made the mistake of bringing up the forbidden subject of the transportation of the Jews. Recently returned from a trip to Amsterdam, she mentioned having observed the rounding up of Jews for transportation. Needless to say, Hitler was not impressed by her having raised the matter, which received a frosty reception resulting in the von Schirachs excusing themselves and leaving immediately thereafter.

Following this event a distinct coolness descended upon the relationship between the two men. Baldur von Schirach survived the war and was sentenced to twenty years at Nuremberg in 1946. Released together with Albert Speer in 1966 von Schirach died at Kröv, a town on the river Mosel in the Rhineland region on 8 August, 1974.

270. Reich Governor Baldur v. Schirach.
This absolutely superb image simply screams the name of 'Hoffmann' from the printed page; it is as fine an example of that Munich photographer's work as can be found. The postmark on the reverse reads; *Wien 17.9.42 Europaeischer Jugendverband Gründungstagung* (Vienna 17.9.42 European Youth Association Foundation Conference).

Reichsstatthalter
BALDUR v. SCHIRACH

Albert Speer

Hitler's brilliant young architect and later Minister for Armaments and Munitions was born to an upper middle class family in Mannheim, on 19 March, 1905. As a student, Speer had wanted to become a mathematician, but was persuaded by his father to follow family tradition and become an architect. Speer studied through the late 1920s at Karlsruhe, Munich and finally Berlin to qualify in the profession chosen for him by his father.

Albert Speer had never been greatly interested in politics, and it was a chance meeting where he and some friends heard Hitler speak at a student gathering in Berlin, in January, 1931 which completely captivated the young man. In 1932, Speer, now with a young wife Margerethe to support, was unemployed, but only temporarily; he received an offer of work via contacts within the NSDAP renovating their local headquarters. This work brought him into occasional contact with Hitler and this led to his being appointed 'unofficial' architect to Hitler.

It has been suggested that Hitler saw many of his own early unsuccessful aspirations fulfilled in Albert Speer. The young architect was to become so highly regarded by the Führer that he was invited to live on the Obersalzberg, joining Goering, Bormann and the other Party *élite* who spent time there. Hitler, frequently 'dropped in' unannounced on Speer and together they would pour over various plans for hours on end. The Führer often presented his own sketches and ideas for discussion at these impromptu meetings and, on occasion even accepted criticism of these from Speer; something Hitler would not easily accept from others. When the two men were together, it was understood that all other business had to wait.

In 1934 Hitler instructed Speer to construct a massive new complex at Nuremberg as a venue

Profes

271. Professor Speer.
Albert Speer as photographed by Hoffmann. Speer turns up frequently in normal 'press type' photographs but postcards of the man are quite rare.

for the Annual Party Rallies. The final area covered a staggering sixteen square kilometres. Speer's imaginative, stage managed night time parades around the new complex were given added impact by the use of flaming torches, flags and banners together with music and numerous searchlights reaching into the night sky to produce a 'cathedral of light'. These awesome, mesmerizing effects impressed not only the German onlookers but also many foreign visitors.

In January 1937, Speer was commissioned with the rebuilding of Berlin with the theme 'The 1000 Year Reich'. Utilizing architectural models which had been produced by 1939, Hitler and Speer would discuss their plans for the new capital to be renamed 'Germania' often, and at great length.

In early 1938 the Führer instructed his architect to build a new Reichs Chancellery. Speer had one year to complete the task. At one point over 8,000 of Germany's best craftsmen were employed on this single project, again using only the finest materials. Hitler occupied the new building in early January, 1939, and was full of praise for the man with a vision equal to his own.

On 8 February, 1942, Dr Fritz Todt, the Minister for Armaments and Munitions was killed in a plane crash on leaving Rastenburg, Hitler's eastern headquarters. The Führer now turned to his efficient young architect, appointing him Todt's successor. Albert Speer again rose to the challenge, and with phenomenal success, production increased in every area under Speer's control, reaching its high point in the summer of 1944, despite increased Allied air raids. As the course of the war turned against Germany, Speer undertook many personal visits to the various fronts encouraging the troops. He also appeared at rallies together with Goebbels during these dark days in attempts to inspire the people.

Towards the end of 1944, Speer came into conflict with other Party leaders over the conduct, and probable outcome of the war. Bormann's ambitious scheming had raised deep concern with Speer, Goebbels and Goering. They could see Hitler becoming further isolated as he slipped more and more under the influence of the sycophantic Bormann, but they could do nothing. On 20 April, 1945, despite the appalling situation in Berlin, Albert Speer visited the Führer's bunker beneath the Reichs Chancellery to celebrate Hitler's fifty-sixth birthday. Early on the morning of 24 April, Speer left Hitler for the last time; the Führer would commit suicide less than one week later.

During his trial at Nuremberg in 1946, Speer remarked; 'I suppose if Hitler ever had a friend, I would have been that friend'. Albert Speer was sentenced to twenty years, all of which he served. He was released from Spandau Prison in 1966. Hitler's former Minister for Armaments and War Production retired to Heidelberg and spent the remainder of his life writing. It has been suggested that at one point Speer was the second most important man in the Third Reich. Through his successful 'central planning' programme he certainly prolonged Germany's ability to continue the war by almost two years. Albert Speer, confidant and friend of Adolf Hitler, died following a heart attack in London on 1 September, 1981; he had travelled to England to take part in a series of interviews with the BBC.

The Obersalzberg: tangible remains today

The numbered sites on the map indicate the locations of buildings from the Nazi period, whether in a complete state or offering identifiable remains only. At the time of writing, with the exception of Hitler's Berghof, now site only with minimal remains and, the former teahouse at Mooslahnerkopf, now a ruin, all sites are clearly identifiable regardless of their current state using the postcards in this book as a reference aid.

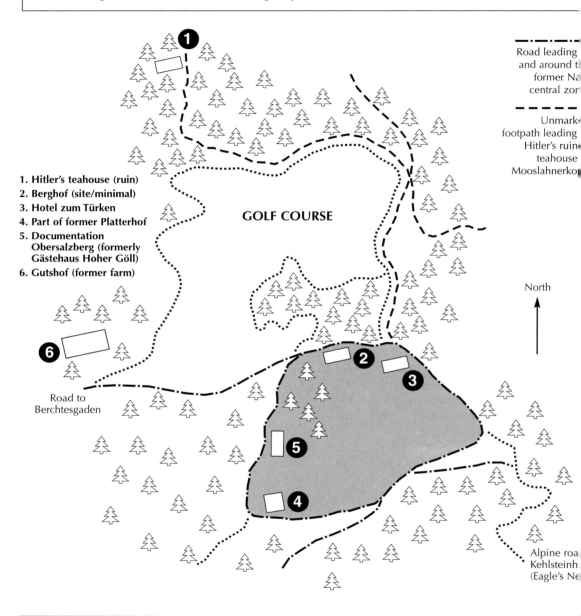

Road leading
and around t
former Na
central zor

Unmark
footpath leading
Hitler's ruin
teahouse
Mooslahnerko

1. Hitler's teahouse (ruin)
2. Berghof (site/minimal)
3. Hotel zum Türken
4. Part of former Platterhof
5. Documentation
   Obersalzberg (formerly
   Gästehaus Hoher Göll)
6. Gutshof (former farm)

GOLF COURSE

North

Road to
Berchtesgaden

Alpine roa
Kehlsteinh
(Eagle's Ne

Shaded area indicates that part of the Obersalzberg to have formed the Nazi central zone.

Indicates location of buildings from the Nazi period whether complete, or site only with some visible remains.

Acknowledgements

While having carried out the research and planning for this book myself, there are those to whom I owe a great deal of thanks for their kind assistance, indulgence and local knowledge, all of which they freely imparted without loosing patience.

A special thank you to;

David Harper, Kurdirektion, Berchtesgaden.

Gerhard Bartels, Bartels Alpenhof, Hintersee, Berchtesgaden.

Finally Lena, for your encouragement and having never complained about the vast amounts of both time and money spent on collecting these postcards over many years; well almost never! For having endured endless hours of neglect while I was totally absorbed on this project, you have my undying devotion.

Bibliography

The following is a list of books which have proved useful in the preparation of this work.

Beierl, Florian M, *History of the Eagle's Nest*, Verlag; Plenk, Berchtesgaden, 2001.

Bullock, Alan, *Hitler a Study in Tyranny*, C. Tinling & Co. Ltd., 1954.
   Originally published by Odhams Press Ltd.

Hanisch, Prof. Dr Ernst, *Obersalzberg, the 'Eagles Nest' and Adolf Hitler*, Berchtesgadener Landesstiftung, 1996.

Hess, Wolf Rüdiger, *My Father Rudolf Hess*, W. H. Allen & Co. Plc, 1987.

Harper, David, *Your Complete Guide to Berchtesgaden*, D. Harper & Ch. Dundas-Harper, Gdbr., 1997.

Semmler, Rudolf, *Goebbels – the man next to Hitler*, John Westhouse (Publishers) Ltd., 1947.

Shirer, William L, *The Rise and Fall of the Third Reich*, Pan Books Ltd., 1964.
   First published by Secker & Warburg, 1960.

Snyder, Louis L, *Encyclopedia of the Third Reich*, The Promotional Reprint Company Ltd., 1995.

Thomas, Hugh, *Hess: A Tale of Two Murders*, Hodder & Stoughton, 1988.

Toland, John, *Adolf Hitler*, Ballantine Books, 1977.

van Capelle, Dr Henk & van de Bovenkamp, Dr Peter, *Hitler's Henchmen*, Warfare (An imprint of Grange Books) 1990.

Appendix

The following information has been taken from the reverse of the postcards shown throughout this book (together with dates of postmarks where these exist). It is offered by way of acknowledgment and credit to the original photographers and publishers of these postcards. This information may be referenced by using the number which relates to each postcard caption.

The reverse of some of the more interesting postcards are also shown on these pages.

1. Photo-Hoffmann, München, Friedrichstr. 34. Echte Fotografie.
2. Photo-Hoffmann, München, Freidrichstr. 34. Echte Fotografie.
3. Alleinvertrieb Walter Preuß, Berlin Friedenau. Stamped: 8.4.38.
4. Eduard Doppler, Braunau am Inn, L&H.
5. Eduard Doppler, Braunau am Inn, L&H. Echte Photographie.
6. Echte Photographie.
7. Photo-Hoffmann, München, Theresienstraße 74. Echt Foto.
8. Photo-Hoffmann, München, Theresienstr. 74. Echte Fotografie.
9. Photo-Hoffmann, München, Theresienstr. 74. Echte Fotografie.
10. Photo-Hoffmann, München, Theresienstr. 74. Echte Fotografie.
11. Max Stadler, Kunstverlag, München, Welfenstrasse 39.
12. Photo-Hoffmann, München, Theresienstr. 74. Echte Fotografie.
13. Ottmar Zieher, München. Fotokarte. Echte Photographie.
14. Südd. Kunstverlag M. Seidlein, München 8. Posted: 2.4.40.
15. A. Lengauer, München. Echte Fotografie.
16. A. Lengauer, München.
17. A. Lengauer, München. Posted: 17.8.36.
18. A. Lengauer, München. Echte Fotografie.
19. Photograph by author.

53

71

20. A. Lengauer, München.
21. A. Lengauer, München. Echte Fotografie. Posted: 12.11.39.
22. Photograph by author.
23. Verlag Carl Krueck, München, Kaufingerstr. 25. Echte Photographie.
Posted:13.5.42.
24. Verlag Carl Krueck, München, Kaufingerstrasse 25. Echtes Foto.
25. Photo-Hoffmann, München, Friedrichstr. 34. Posted: 27.6.40.
26. Photograph by author.
27. Photokarte v. H. Gürtler, Salzburg, Faberstraße 30.
28. Photograph by author.
29. Not credited, reverse unmarked. Posted: 24.1.23.
30. Aufnahme und Verlag F. G. Zeitz, Königssee / Obb. Posted: 12.9.42.
31. Photograph by author.
32. Verlag: L. Ammon, Schönau-Berchtesgaden.
33. Alpiner Kunstverlag Hans Huber, Garmisch-Partenkirchen. Deutsche Heimatbilder.
    Posted: 16.9.41.
34. Verlag: L. Ammon, Schönau-B'gaden. Posted: 14.8.41.
35. Verlag von Karl Ermisch, Berchtesgaden.
36. Verlag von Karl Ermisch, Berchtesgaden.
37. Orig.-Aufn. v. Hans Huber, Alpiner Verlag, Garmisch-Partenkirchen.
    Deutsche Heimatbilder.
38. Gebirgsaufnahme von Michel Lochner, Berchtesgaden.
    No postmark but dated: 14.7.29.
39. L Monopol, Kunst u. Verlagsanstalt A. G. Schöllhorn, München-Innsbruck.
    Posted: 22.8.35.
40. Verlag A. Gg. Schöllhorn München 2. S O. Echte Photographie.
41. Photo-Hoffmann, München, Theresienstr. 74.
42. Photo-Hoffmann, München, Theresienstr. 74.
43. Photo-Hoffmann, München, Theresienstr. 74.
44. Photo-Hoffmann, München, Theresienstr. 74.

45. Photo-Hoffmann, München, Theresienstr. 74.
46. Photo-Hoffmann, München, Theresienstr. 74.
47. Photo-Hoffmann, München, Theresienstr. 74.
48. Photo-Hoffmann, München, Theresienstr. 74.
49. Photo-Hoffmann, München, Theresienstr. 74.
50. Alpiner Kunstverlag Hans Huber München 19. Deutsche Heimatbilder.
51. Freig. D. Prüfst d. R.L.M. Hersteller: Helff & Stein GMBH, Leipzig C 1.
    Echte Fotografie.
52. Orig.-Aufnahme Kunst und Verlagsanstalt Martin Herpich, München.
    Echte Photographie.
53. Not credited, reverse unmarked. Posted: 21.8.33.
54. Kunstverlag Friedrich Schmidt jr., Frankfurt a. M., Kleiner Hirschgraben 11.
    Photo Reinelt. Echte Fotografie.
55. Heinrich Hoffmann, Verlag Nationalsozialistischer Bilder, Düsseldorf, Wilhelmplatz 12.
Echte Fotografie.
56. Verlag: Theodor Fritsch jun., Leipzig C 1. Ges. gesch. Bromüra.
57. Foto Böhm, Verlag Michael Lochner, Berchtesgaden. Posted: 29.12.33.
58. Gebirgsaufnahmen von Michael Lochner, Berchtesgaden. Echte Fotografie.
59. Photo-Hoffmann, Berlin SW 68, Kochstr. 10.
60. Graph. Kunst und Verlagsanstalt Jos. C. Huber, Diessen vor München.
    Phot. E. Schmauß, München.
61. Aufnahme von Michael Lochner, Berchtesgaden. Echte Fotografie.
62. Alpiner Kunstverlag Hans Huber, München 19. Deutsche Heimatbilder.
63. Photograph by author.
64. Photo-Hoffmann, München, Theresienstr. 74. Echte Fotografie.
65. Alpiner Kunstverlag Hans Huber, München 19. Deutsche Heimatbilder.
66. Photohaus J. Schmid, Berchtesgaden, Fernruf 254. Echt Photo.
67. Alpiner Kunstverlag Hans Huber, München 19. Deutsche Heimatbilder.
    Posted: 27.7.33.
68. Aufn. u. Verlag M. Lochner, Obersalzberg, Berchtesgaden. Posted: 10.9.35.

90

Rear jacket (bottom)

69. Cosy Verlag, A. Gründler, Freilassing. Echte Photographie. Posted: 1934.
70. Cosy Verlag, Alfred Gründler, Zweigstelle Freilassing. Posted: 26.5.35.
71. Photo-Hoffmann, München, Theresienstr. 74. Posted: 9.9.34.
72. Photo-Hoffmann, Berlin SW 68, Kochstr. 10.
73. Alpiner Kunstverlag Hans Huber, München 19. Deutsche Heimatbilder. Posted: 16.6.34.
74. Verlag: L. Ammon, Schönau-B'gaden. Echte Fotografie.
75. Verlag von Karl Ermisch, Berchtesgaden. Posted: 8.8.35.
76. Photo Brandner, unterhalb Haus Wachenfeld, Telef. 83. Echt Foto.
77. Photo-Hoffmann, München, Friedrichstr. 34. Echte Fotografie.
78. Verlag von Karl Ermisch, Berchtesgaden. Posted: 1935.
79. Photo-Hoffmann, Berlin SW 68, Kochstr. 10.
80. Photo-Hoffmann, München, Theresienstr. 74. Echte Fotografie.
81. Photo-Hoffmann München Friedrichstr. 34. Echte Fotografie.
82. Alpiner Kunstverlag Hans Huber, Garmisch-Partenkirchen. Deutsche Heimatbilder. Posted: 11.6.35.
83. Aufnahme und Verlag v. M. Lochner, Berchtesgaden. Echte Photographie.
84. Gebirgsaufnahmen von Michael Lochner, Berchtesgaden. Echte Fotografie.
85. Photo-Hoffmann, München, Theresienstr. 74. Uvachrom.
86. Orig.-Aufn. v. Hans Huber. Alpiner Verlag, Garmisch-Partenkirchen. Deutsche Heimatbilder. Posted: 1.8.35.
87. Orig.-Aufn. v. Hans Huber, Alpiner Verlag, München 19.
88. Photo-Hoffmann, München, Theresienstr. 74. Uvachrom.
89. Photo-Hoffmann, München, Friedrichstr. 34. Echte Fotografie.
90. Photo-Hoffmann, München, Friedrichstr. 34. Stamped: 30.9.38.
91. Photo-Hoffmann, München, Amalienstr. 25. Uvachrom.
92. Photo-Hoffmann, München, Friedrichstr. 34. Echte Fotografie.
93. Photo-Hoffmann, München, Theresienstr. 74. Echte Fotografie.
94. Photo-Hoffmann, München, Amalienstr. 25. Uvachrom.

95. Photo-Hoffmann, München, Theresienstr. 74. Uvachrom.
96. Photo-Hoffmann, München, Theresienstr. 74. Uvachrom.
97. Photo-Hoffmann, München, Theresienstr. 74. Echte Photographie.
98. Photo-Hoffmann, München, Theresienstr. 74. Uvachrom.
99. Photo-Hoffmann, München, Theresienstr. 74. Uvachrom-Aufnahme. Posted 29.5.37.
100. Photo-Hoffmann, München, Theresienstr. 74.
101. Photo Jul. Hillebrand, Königssee (Ob.-Bayern). Echt Foto.
102. Photo-Hoffmann München Theresienstr. 74. Echte Fotografie.
103. Photo-Hoffmann, München, Friedrichstr. 34. Echte Fotografie.
     Not posted but dated: 6.9.43.
104. Rudolf Schneider-Verlag. Reichenau (Ga.). Aufn. P. J. Hoffmann.
105. Photo-Hoffmann, München, Friedrichstraße 34. Echte Fotografie.
106. Orig.-Aufnahme Kunst und Verlagsanstalt Martin Herpich, München. Echte Fotografie.
107. Aufnahme und Verlag: M. Lochner, Berchtesgaden. Echte Photographie.
108. Photohaus J. Schmid, Berchtesgaden, Fernruf 254. Echt Foto.
109. Photo-Hoffmann, München, Friedrichstr. 34. Posted: 6.12.42.
110. Cosy-Verlag, Salzburg, Getreidgasse 22. Echte Photographie.
111. Verlag: L. Ammon, Schönau-B'gaden. Posted: 22.10.36.
112. Bilddruck der Rückseite: Brendamour, Simhart & Co. München.
     Commerorative stamp dated: 20.4.41
113. Verlag L. Ammon, Berchtesgaden-Schönau. Echte Photographie.
114. Aufnahme und Verlag F. G. Zeitz, Königssee Obb. Echte Photographie.
115. Photo-Hoffmann, München, Theresienstr. 74. Echte Fotografie.
116. Photo-Hoffmann, München, Friedrichstr. 34. Echte Fotografie.
117. Photo-Hoffmann, München, Theresienstr. 74. Echte Fotografie.
118. Photo-Hoffmann, München, Theresienstr. 74. Echte Fotografie.
119. Photohaus J. Schmid, Berchtesgaden, Fernruf 254. Posted: 13.7.37.
120. Aufnahme und Verlag F. G. Zeitz, Königssee / Obb. Posted: 25.10.38.

112

121. Photo-Hoffmann, München, Friedrichstr. 34. Echte Fotografie.
122. Aufnahme und Verlag F. G. Zeitz, Königssee / Obb. Original Zeitz-Photo.
123. Photo-Hoffmann, München, Theresienstr. 74.
     Commemorative postmark: 10.4.38 (Plebiscite on reunion of Austria
     and the German Reich).
124. Photohaus J. Schmid, Berchtesgaden, Fernruf 254. Posted: 18.9.37.
125. Photohaus J. Schmid, Berchtesgaden, Fernruf 254. Echt Photo.
126. Verlag Photo Böhm, Deutsche Buchhandlung, Berchtesgaden. Echt Foto.
127. Photohaus J. Schmid, Berchtesgaden – Fernruf 254. Posted: 16.1.41.
128. Orig.-Aufn. v. Hans Huber, Alpiner Verlag, Garmisch-Partenkirchen.
     Deutsche Heimatbilder.
129. Aufnahme und Verlag M. Lochner, Berchtesgaden. Echte Photographie.
130. Photo-Haus J. Schmid, Berchtesgaden. Echte Photographie.
131. Photograph by author.
132. Photograph by author.
133. Photograph by author.
134. Aufnahme und Verlag F. G. Zeitz, Konigssee / Obb. Posted: 18.8.41.
135. Deutsche Kunst und Verlagsanstalt, G.m.b.H., Dortmund, Stubengasse 29.
     Posted: 6.10.42.
136. Photo-Hoffmann, München, Friedrichstr. 34. Echte Fotografie.
137. Photo-Hoffmann, München, Friedrichstr. 34. Echte Fotografie.
138. Verlag M. Bauer, München 13. Echt Foto.
139. Verlag M. Bauer, München 13. Echt Foto.
140. Verlag M. Bauer, München 13. Echt Foto.
141. Photo-Hoffmann, München, Friedrichstr. 34. Echte Fotografie.
142. Verlag Heinrich Hoffmann, München. Not posted but dated: 3.6.43.
143. Verlag Heinrich Hoffmann, München.
144. Photo-Hoffmann, München, Friedrichstr. 34. Echte Fotografie.
145. Photo-Hoffmann, München, Friedrichstr. 34. Echte Fotografie.

146. Photo-Hoffmann, München, Theresienstr. 74. Echte Fotografie.
147. Photo-Hoffmann, München, Friedrichstr. 34. Echte Fotografie.
148. Verlag Heinrich Hoffmann, München.
149. Verlag M. Bauer, München 13. Echt Foto.
150. Photo-Hoffmann, München, Theresienstr. 74. Echte Fotografie.
151. Photo-Hoffmann, München, Friedrichstraße 34. Vitacolor.
152. Photo-Hoffmann, München, Theresienstr. 74. Posted: 1.7.37.
153. Photo-Hoffmann, München, Theresienstr. 74. Echte Fotografie.
154. Köhler-Tiftze Bad Elster. Ergo.
155. Photo-Hoffmann, München, Theresienstr. 74. Echte Fotografie.
156. Photo-Hoffmann, München, Theresienstr. 74. Echte Fotografie.
157. Photo-Hoffmann, München, Theresienstr. 74. Echte Fotografie.
158. Photo-Hoffmann, München, Theresienstr. 74. Echte Photographie.
159. Aufnahme und Verlag F. G. Zeitz, Königssee / Obb. Posted: 26.8.34.
160. Photo-Hoffmann, München, Friedrichstr. 34. Echte Fotografie.
161. Photo-Hoffmann, München, Theresienstr. 74. Posted: 19.10.38.
162. Photo-Pfingstl, Berchtesgaden. Aufgenommen auf Agfa Isochrom-Film.
163. Photo-Hoffmann, München, Theresienstr. 74. Echte Fotografie.
164. Photo-Hoffmann, München, Friedrichstr. 34. Echte Fotografie.
165. Photo-Hoffmann, München, Theresienstr. 74. Echte Fotografie.
166. Photo-Hoffmann, München, Theresienstr. 74. Echte Fotografie.
167. Alpiner Kunstverlag Hans Huber, München. Deutsche Heimatbilder.
     Posted: 5.10.33.
168. Photo-Hoffmann, München, Friedrichstr. 34. Posted: 14.5.40.
169. Photo-Hoffmann, München, Theresienstr. 74.
170. Photo-Hoffmann, München, Theresienstr. 74. Echte Fotografie.
171. Photo-Hoffmann, München, Theresienstr. 74. Echte Fotografie.
172. Photo-Hoffmann, München, Theresienstr. 74. Echte Fotografie.
173. Photo-Hoffmann, München, Amalienstr. 25. Echt Photo.

183

198. Deutsche Kunst und Verlagsanstalt, G.m.b.H., Dortmund, Stubengasse 29. Echte Fotografie.
199. Deutsche Kunst und Verlagsanstalt, G.m.b.H., Dortmund, Stubengasse 29. Echte Fotografie.
200. Deutsche Kunst und Verlagsanstalt, G.m.b.H., Dortmund, Stubengasse 29. Echte Fotografie.
201. Deutsche Kunst und Verlagsanstalt, G.m.b.H., Dortmund, Stubengasse 29. Echte Fotografie.
202. Deutsche Kunst und Verlagsanstalt, G.m.b.H., Dortmund, Stubengasse 29. Posted: 2.12.42.
203. Deutsche Kunst und Verlagsanstalt, G.m.b.H., Dortmund, Stubengasse 29. Echte Fotografie.
204. Deutsche Kunst und Verlagsanstalt, G.m.b.H., Dortmund, Stubengasse 29. Posted: 8.6.44.
205. Deutsche Kunst und Verlagsanstalt, G.m.b.H., Dortmund, Stubengasse 29. Echte Fotografie.
206. Ross Verlag. Foto Clausen.
207. Alpiner Kunstverlag Hans Huber, Garmisch-Partenkirchen. Deutsche Heimatbilder.
208. Photo-Hoffmann, München, Friedrichstr. 34. Echte Fotografie.
209. Aufnahme und Verlag: M. Lochner, Berchtesgaden. Echte Photographie.
210. Ross Verlag. Foto Clausen. Posted: 10.7.40.
211. Verlag: L. Ammon, Schönau-B'gaden. Echte Fotografie.
212. Cosy-Verlag, Salzburg, Getreidegasse 22. Echte Photographie.
213. Foto Rosemarie Clausen. Ross-Verlag, Berlin SW 68. Posted: 7.2.41.
214. Aufnahme und Verlag U. Bornemann, Blankenburg-Harz. Echte Photographie.
215. Photo-Hoffmann, München, Theresienstr. 74.
216. Photo-Hoffmann, München, Theresienstr. 74.
217. Photo-Hoffmann, München, Theresienstr. 74.
218. Photo-Hoffmann, München, Theresienstr. 74.

204

247

219. Photohaus J. Schmid, Berchtesgaden. Tel. 254. Posted: 18.7.32.
220. Photo-Hoffmann, München, Friedrichstr. 34. Echte Fotografie.
221. L. Monopol, Kunst u. Verlagsanstalt A. G. Schöllhorn. München-Innsbruck. Echte Fotografie.
222. Aufnahme und Verlag: M. Lochner, Berchtesgaden. Echte Photographie.
223. Not credited, reverse unmarked.
224. Ansichtskartenfabrik Schöning & Co., Lübeck. Echte Fotografie.
225. Ansichtskartenfabrik Schöning & Co., Lübeck. Echte Fotografie.
226. Aufnahme u. Verlag: F. G. Zeitz, Königssee/Obb. Original-Zeitz-Photo.
227. Alpiner Kunstverlag Hans Huber, Garmisch-Partenkirchen.
228. Alpiner Kunstverlag Hans Huber, Garmisch-Partenkirchen.
229. Privately taken photograph, source unknown, reverse unmarked.
230. Privately taken photograph, source unknown, reverse unmarked.
231. Privately taken photograph, source unknown, reverse unmarked.
232. Privately taken photograph, source unknown, reverse unmarked.
233. Privately taken photograph, source unknown, reverse unmarked.
234. Privately taken photograph, source unknown, reverse unmarked.
235. Privately taken photograph, source unknown, reverse unmarked.
236. Privately taken photograph, source unknown, reverse unmarked.
237. Privately taken photograph, source unknown, reverse unmarked.
238. Privately taken photograph, source unknown, reverse unmarked.
239. Privately taken photograph, source unknown, reverse unmarked.
240. Privately taken photograph, source unknown, reverse unmarked.
241. Verlag: L. Ammon, Schönau-B'gaden.
242. Photograph by author.
243. Aufnahme und Verlag: M. Lochner, Berchtesgaden. Echte Photographie. Posted: 8.12.40.
244. Aufnahme und Verlag: M. Lochner, Berchtesgaden. Echte Photographie. Posted: 10.9.40.

245. Aufnahme Dr. Wiedemann. Herausgegeben vom Generalkommando VII. A.K.
246. Photograph by author.
247. Aufnahme und Verlag M. Lochner, Berchtesgaden. Echte Photographie.
Posted: 22.5.42.
248. Kunst u. Verlagsanstalt Martin Herpich, München. Foto Karl Kruse,
Bad Reichenhall – Kirchberg. Freigegeben d. RLM. 5.4.35. Posted 29.10.39.
249. Aufnahme und Verlag F. G. Zeitz, Königssee / Obb. Original-Zeitz-Photo.
250. Photohaus J. Schmid, Berchtesgaden, Fernruf 254. Posted: 28.1.39.
251. Aufnahme und Verlag: M. Lochner, Berchtesgaden. Echte Photographie.
252. Verlag: L. Ammon, Schönau-B'gaden.
253. Photograph by author.
254. Reichs-Bildberichterstatter der NSDAP, Heinrich Hoffmann.
255. Photo-Hoffmann, München, Theresienstraße 74.
256. Privately taken photograph, source unknown, reverse unmarked.
257. Photo-Hoffmann, München, Theresienstr. 74. Echte Fotografie.
258. Phot. Rob. Röhr. Echte Photographie.
259. Not credited, reverse unmarked.
260. Photo-Hoffmann, München, Friedrichstr. 34. Echte Fotografie.
261. Sandau, Berlin. Film-Foto-Verlag, Berlin SW68. Echt Photo.
262. Film-Foto-Verlag, Berlin SW68. Zur Veröffentlichung freigegeben.
Foto Rosemarie Clausen.
263. Photo-Hoffmann, München, Theresienstr. 74. Echte Fotografie.
264. Photo-Hoffmann, München, Amalienstr. 25. Echte Photographie.
265. Photo-Hoffmann, München, Friedrichstr. 34. Echte Fotografie.
266. Phot. Rob. Röhr, Magdeburg. Echte Photographie.
267. Phot. u. Verlag Rob. Röhr, Magdeburg. Echte Photographie.
268. Contemporary official stamp on reverse reads;
SS Panzer Grenadier Regiment 'Der Führer'.
269. Atelier Kiesel, Berlin phot. Verlag Ross Berlin SW 68.
270. Photo-Hoffmann, München, Friedrichstr. 34. Posted: 17.9.42.
271. Photo-Hoffmann, München, Friedrichstr. 34. Echte Fotografie.
Not posted but date stamped: 6.6.43.

Jacket images (front).

Top right: After an original painting by Willy Exner.
                Photo-Hoffmann, München, Friedrichstr. 34.
Main image: Adolf Hitler's country house on Obersalzberg near Berchtesgaden.
                DrTPo.

Jacket images (back).

Main image: (see also page 12).
                Reichs-Bildberichterstatter der NSDAP, Heinrich Hoffmann.
Middle left: Berghof Wachenfeld country house of the Reichs Chancellor in Berchtesgaden.
                Photo-Hoffmann, München, Theresienstr. 74.
Middle right: (see also page 13).
                Verlag Heinrich Hoffmann, München.
Bottom: Berghof Wachenfeld country house of the Reichs Chancellor in Berchtesgaden.
                Photo-Hoffmann, München, Theresienstr. 74.

Images used on pages 6/7 and 8/9.

                Fot. Ernst Baumann, Bad Reichenhall.